— THE NEW —

Bundt Pan

COOKBOOK

BY THE EDITORS OF *TIDE & TOWN*

CIDER MILL
PRESS

BOOK
PUBLISHERS
KENNEBUNKPORT, MAINE

13-Digit ISBN: 978-1604337402
10-Digit ISBN: 1604337400

This book may be ordered by mail from the publisher. Please include $5.99 for postage and handling.
Please support your local bookseller first!

Books published by Cider Mill Press Book Publishers are available at special discounts for bulk purchases in the United States by corporations, institutions, and other organizations. For more information, please contact the publisher.

Cider Mill Press Book Publishers
"Where good books are ready for press"
PO Box 454
12 Spring Street
Kennebunkport, Maine 04046

Visit us on the Web! www.cidermillpress.com

Design by Cindy Butler

Typography: AdageScript, Avenir, Burford Base, Helvetica, Brandon Printed
All images are used under official license from Shutterstock.com

Printed in China
1 2 3 4 5 6 7 8 9 0
First Edition

Table of Contents

Introduction

With limited cabinet space and a limited budget, we're all used to finding creative ways to use ordinary tools to extraordinary ends. Everyone hates a unitasker. Moping, taking up valuable shelf real estate, glaring at you reproachfully from behind your favored alternatives as you pass it by time and time again.

For many of us, this character may be played by a true classic: the Bundt pan. Gawky, highly decorative, with its distinctive empty center, it might not seem a naturally versatile piece of equipment. Maybe you group it together with other one-trick ponies, like the ice cream machine from your wedding registry or the huge dull cleaver inherited from a bygone roommate.

Talk about miscasting! The Bundt pan has got plenty of undeniable advantages. For one thing, there are tons of them floating around. Some estimates put it as the most ubiquitous pan in the *world*, so odds are you already have one or two. And if you don't, $3 and a five-minute trip to any garage sale in the country will solve that problem for you.

And once you experiment a bit, you might realize that the Bundt pan offers a home cook so much more than you expected.

The History of the Bundt Pan

For centuries, bakeries in Eastern and Central Europe have made marble cakes whose shapes resemble the famous Bundt mold we know today. The cake, called *kugelhopf*, was usually made for special occasions like weddings or town socials; like most marbles, it was often customized with a number of familiar ingredients—chocolate, dried fruit or poppy seeds, to name a few. As to the cake's specific region of origin, historians disagree. And they aren't the only ones. Turks, Germans, Austrians, French—all claim to have birthed the famous cake, and with great fervor. Wherever it began, bakers across the continent relied on beautiful pottery molds to give it its unique shape, rather than the aluminum pans of today.

In fact, the aluminum Bundt pan didn't arrive on the scene until 1950; unsurprisingly, it was invented for the expressed purpose of baking a *kugelhopf.* H. David Dalquist, owner of a Minnesota-based kitchenware company called Nordic Ware, used his newly created pan to bake a *kugelhopf* for the Hadassah Society—an international organization for Jewish women. Though he originally called his creation the "bund pan," Dalquist eventually changed the name.

Despite Dalquist's success, the Bundt pan toiled away in relative obscurity for the next 16 years. Everything changed in 1966, when a "Tunnel of Fudge" Bundt Cake placed second in the annual Pillsbury Bake-Off. Suddenly the Bundt had a national stage—and a rush of orders soon followed. Before long, Dalquist's company was making upwards of 30,000 pans a day, explaining the pan's ubiquity in households across the country today. In fact, *Food & Wine* estimates that more than 70 million households currently have Bundt pans. Not bad for a centuries-old cake mold of vague origin!

Care and Use

Bundt pans come in all manner of sizes, designs and material, each with the same potential issue: sticking. The elaborate patterns on the surface of the pan create a tendency for food to stick, so in many cases you will be instructed to carefully grease the pan with canola oil spray. Make sure you heed these directions—nothing feels worse than expecting to turn out a cake and leaving half of it stuck to the pan.

If you're not lucky enough to inherit a pan and need to buy one, pay attention to the manufacturer's directions beforehand. For instance, many newer pans with nonstick surfaces do not recommend metal utensils, since they may scratch off the coating. As for the material of the pan itself, we've found in general that heavier metal pans cook more evenly, produce better browning and turn out more clearly than their plastic or acrylic counterparts. That said, these recipes are designed for every Bundt pan under the sun! Just be sure to grease acrylic pans extra carefully.

The number one rule for treating your Bundt pan right?
Use it as often as you can!

Bundt Pan Shapes

Bundt pans come in all shapes and sizes. Though some are more intricately designed than others, all Bundt pans and cakes have a recognizable center hole that sets them apart from other baking pans. More often than not, the different designs are simply a matter of decorative taste. However, some recipes, such as sponge cakes, are more suited to simpler or flat pans because their light batter easily sticks to pans with too many ridges.

With so many different decorative options available, no two are alike. A "standard" Bundt usually holds about 12 cups, and a mini Bundt pan usually holds about 4 cups. If your pans are different, don't fret! Turn to page 215 for more information about using different pan sizes.

CLASSIC This shape is the most recognizable, with its rounded ridges. When turned over, it produces the iconic round dome.

SQUARE What's unique about this Bundt is that, unlike other pans, this cake is a perfect square. But, it still has the same center opening as its circular relatives.

SWIRL This style Bundt pan is so mesmerizing that it barely needs a topping. Its swirl shape has led this pan to be called a Hurricane Bundt.

FLAT The flat Bundt is more suited for recipes that will easily stick to ridges, or recipes that need a flat top for decorative frosting. There are varieties of this pan that come with a spring release for easy removal.

STAR, HONEYCOMB, OR DIAMOND CUT This Bundt is easily recognized by its sharp-edged ridges, giving it a geometric look. This pan is better for heartier fillings that can withstand all those intricate grooves.

CATHEDRAL OR FLEUR DE LIS Possibly the most beautiful of Bundt pans, the cathedral style pan has dome edges and intricate designs that mimic the high ceilings and stained-glass windows of a cathedral.

Breakfast

Breakfast is considered the most important meal of the day, but trying to feed a crowd can also make it the most tedious meals. A Bundt pan is the easiest way to take your brunch to the next level with a decorative presentation and great group portions. Imagine serving your friends a giant Lemon Poppyseed Muffin Cake (page 41) or Vegetable Frittata (page 44). A ring of Maple Bacon Sticky Buns (page 21) would make anyone's mouth water, and Mini Bundt Pan Doughnuts (page 34) make it easier than ever to have fresh, baked doughnuts at home.

—STICKY BUNS—

TIME: 90 MINUTES   SERVES: 6

This takes a bit of preparation time, but the result is worth it! Cooking in a Bundt pan makes a gooey ring of pull-apart rolls. For a beautiful display, make a batch of Vanilla Glaze (page 188), pour it in a small bowl, and place the bowl in the center of the ring. Everyone can add as much as they like to their roll! For easy cleanup, line your Bundt pan with parchment paper.

1 (26.4-OZ.) PACKAGE FROZEN BISCUITS

ALL-PURPOSE FLOUR, FOR DUSTING

2 TEASPOONS GROUND CINNAMON

¾ CUP FIRMLY PACKED DARK BROWN SUGAR

4 TABLESPOONS BUTTER, SOFTENED

POWDERED SUGAR OR VANILLA GLAZE (PAGE 188), FOR SERVING

1) Preheat the oven to 375 degrees.

2) Lightly dust a flat surface with flour. Spread the frozen biscuit dough out in rows of 4 biscuits each. Cover with a dish cloth and let sit for about 30 minutes until the dough is thawed but still cool.

3) Mix the brown sugar and cinnamon in a small bowl.

4) When the dough is ready, sprinkle flour over the top and fold it in half, then press it out to form a large rectangle (approximately 10x12 inches). Spread the softened butter over the dough, then the cinnamon/sugar mix. Roll up the dough, starting with a long side. Cut into 1-inch slices.

5) Thoroughly coat your Bundt pan with butter or cooking spray to prevent sticking, or layer the bottom with parchment paper. Layer the slices along the bottom of the Bundt pan, with the swirled side facing up. If not all of the slices will rest flat, slightly overlap the slices on one side.

6) Bake at 375 degrees for about 35 minutes, until rolls are cooked through in the center. Remove from the oven and allow to cool slightly.

7) Dust with powdered sugar or Vanilla Glaze (page 188).

—MAPLE BACON STICKY BUNS—

TIME: 2 HOURS   SERVES: 6

This spin on traditional sticky buns combines the sticky-sweet texture of maple syrup with the salty taste of bacon. Although you could grease the pan with butter or cooking spray, the maple syrup is extra sticky, making parchment paper a better option for both removal and cleanup. Don't worry, your buns will still have the beautiful ring shape of the Bundt Pan!

1 (26.4-OZ.) PACKAGE FROZEN BISCUITS

ALL-PURPOSE FLOUR FOR DUSTING

¼ POUND BACON (ABOUT 6 SLICES), COOKED AND CRUMBLED

4 TABLESPOONS BUTTER, SOFTENED

¼ CUP MAPLE SYRUP

¾ CUP FIRMLY PACKED LIGHT BROWN SUGAR

POWDERED SUGAR OR VANILLA GLAZE (PAGE 188), FOR SERVING

1) Preheat the oven to 375 degrees.

2) Lightly dust a flat surface with flour. Spread the frozen biscuit dough out in rows of 4 biscuits each. Cover with a dish cloth and let sit for about 30 minutes until the dough is thawed but still cool.

3) Sprinkle flour over the top of the biscuit dough, and fold the dough in half, then press it out to form a large rectangle (approximately 10 inches by 12 inches). Spread the softened butter over the dough.

4) In a bowl, combine the maple syrup with the brown sugar. Spread the mixture on the dough over the butter. Sprinkle the crumbles bacon over the dough.

5) Roll the dough with the butter, maple syrup mixture, and bacon in it, starting with a long side. Cut into 1-inch slices.

6) Line your Bundt with parchment paper to prevent sticking. Layer the slices along the bottom of the Bundt pan, with the swirled side facing up. If not all of the slices will rest flat, slightly overlap the slices on one side.

7) Bake at 375 degrees for about 35 minutes, until the rolls are cooked through. Remove from the oven and allow to cool.

—CRANBERRY WALNUT STICKY BUNS—

TIME: 2 HOURS   SERVES: 6

The tartness of cranberries is the perfect balance to walnuts in these perfectly sweet sticky buns. For a fantastic display, prepare one recipe of Vanilla Glaze (page 188), pour it in a bowl, and place it in the center of the ring of sticky buns before serving. If you're worried about cleanup, use parchment paper to line your Bundt pan before placing the dough in the pan.

1 (26.4-OZ.) PACKAGE FROZEN BISCUITS

ALL-PURPOSE FLOUR FOR DUSTING

4 TABLESPOONS BUTTER, SOFTENED

¾ CUP FIRMLY PACKED LIGHT BROWN SUGAR

1 TEASPOON GROUND CINNAMON

½ CUP CHOPPED WALNUTS

½ CUP HALVED CRANBERRIES

POWDERED SUGAR OR VANILLA GLAZE (PAGE 188), FOR SERVING

1) Preheat the oven to 375 degrees.

2) Lightly dust a flat surface with flour. Spread the frozen biscuit dough out in rows of 4 biscuits each. Cover with a dish cloth and let sit for about 30 minutes until the dough is thawed but still cool.

3) Sprinkle flour over the top of the biscuit dough, and fold the dough in half, then press it out to form a large rectangle (approximately 10 inches by 12 inches). Spread the softened butter over the dough.

4) Sprinkle the brown sugar and cinnamon over the butter, then add the walnuts and cranberries. Roll the dough with a long side. Cut into 1-inch slices.

5) Thoroughly coat your Bundt pan with butter or cooking spray to prevent sticking, or layer the bottom with parchment paper. Layer the slices along the bottom of the Bundt pan, with the swirled side facing up. If not all of the slices will rest flat, slightly overlap the slices on one side.

6) Bake at 375 degrees for about 35 minutes, until the rolls are cooked through. Remove from the oven and allow to cool.

7) Dust with powdered sugar or Vanilla Glaze (page 188).

—STREUSEL SWIRLED CINNAMON COFFEE CAKE—

TIME: 60 MINUTES   MAKES: 8–10

Add this no-frills coffee cake to an intricately designed Bundt pan and blow your guests away without breaking a sweat. Even better: The chances are very high that everything you need is already in your pantry!

1 ½ CUPS BUTTER, ROOM TEMPERATURE

1 ½ CUPS SUGAR

3 EGGS, ROOM TEMPERATURE

1 ½ TEASPOONS VANILLA EXTRACT

1 ¼ CUPS SOUR CREAM

2 ½ CUPS ALL-PURPOSE FLOUR

2 TEASPOONS BAKING POWDER

½ TEASPOON SALT

FOR THE STREUSEL FILLING:

1 CUP BROWN SUGAR

1 ½ TABLESPOONS CINNAMON

1 TEASPOON COCOA POWDER

FOR THE GLAZE:

1 CUP POWDERED SUGAR

2 TABLESPOONS WHOLE MILK

1) Preheat oven to 350 degrees. Liberally coat the Bundt pan with butter or canola oil spray and lightly flour, tapping out the excess flour to create a thin, even coat.

2) In a stand mixer with a paddle attachment, cream together the butter and sugar until the mixture is light and fluffy. Once finished, add the eggs one at a time and beat until thoroughly incorporated, scraping down the sides of the bowl after each egg. Add the vanilla extract, followed by the sour cream.

3) In a separate, medium mixing bowl, combine flour, baking powder, and salt.

4) Add the flour mixture to the egg mixture and mix briefly—just enough to incorporate all ingredients.

5) Transfer mixture to the prepared Bundt pan and spread batter evenly throughout the pan.

6) For the streusel, mix together brown sugar, cinnamon, and cocoa powder in a small mixing bowl. Pour over the top of the cake batter, then use a butter knife to swirl the streusel into the cake batter.

7) Bake at 350 for 45-50 minutes or until a toothpick comes out mostly clean.

8) Allow the cake to rest in the pan for up to 30 minutes, then turn out of the pan and allow to completely cool on a wire cooling rack.

9) While the cake cools, whisk together the powdered sugar and 2 tablespoons of milk to make the glaze. When the cake is mostly cool and has been turned out of the pan, use a whisk to drizzle the glaze over it.

—MOCHA SWIRL COFFEE CAKE—

TIME: 60 MINUTES   SERVES: 8–10

This cake takes the phrase "coffee cake" seriously with a delicious mocha swirl running through it. You won't even need a morning cup of coffee with this sweet treat!

1 ½ CUPS BUTTER, ROOM TEMPERATURE

1 ½ CUPS SUGAR

3 EGGS, ROOM TEMPERATURE

1 ½ TEASPOONS VANILLA EXTRACT

1 ¼ CUPS SOUR CREAM

2 ½ CUPS ALL-PURPOSE FLOUR

2 TEASPOONS BAKING POWDER

1 TABLESPOON COCOA POWDER

½ TEASPOON SALT

FOR THE MOCHA SWIRL:

2 TEASPOONS VANILLA EXTRACT

2 TABLESPOONS ESPRESSO POWDER OR INSTANT COFFEE

¼ CUP CHOCOLATE CHIPS

FOR THE GLAZE:

1 CUP POWDERED SUGAR

2 TABLESPOONS WHOLE MILK

1 TEASPOON ESPRESSO POWDER OR INSTANT COFFEE

1) Preheat oven to 350 degrees. Liberally coat the Bundt pan with butter or canola oil spray and lightly flour, tapping out the excess flour to create a thin, even coat.

2) In a stand mixer with a paddle attachment, cream together the butter and sugar until the mixture is light and fluffy. Once finished, add the eggs one at a time and beat until thoroughly incorporated, scraping down the sides of the bowl after each egg. Add the vanilla extract, followed by the sour cream.

3) In a separate, medium mixing bowl, combine flour, baking powder, cocoa powder, and salt.

4) Add the flour mixture to the egg mixture and mix briefly—just enough to incorporate all ingredients.

5) Transfer mixture to the prepared Bundt pan and spread batter evenly throughout the pan.

6) For the mocha swirl, mix together the vanilla, espresso, and chocolate chips in a small mixing bowl. Pour over the top of the cake batter, then use a butter knife to swirl the streusel into the cake batter.

7) Bake at 350 for 45-50 minutes or until a toothpick comes out mostly clean.

8) Allow the cake to rest in the pan for up to 30 minutes, then turn out of the pan and allow to completely cool on a wire cooling rack.

9) While the cake cools, whisk together the powdered sugar, milk, and espresso to make the glaze. When the cake is mostly cool and has been turned out of the pan, use a whisk to drizzle the glaze over it.

For Added
SWEETNESS

IF YOU'D LIKE TO ADD EVEN MORE SWEETNESS
TO THIS CAKE, SUBSTITUTE THE PEANUTS FOR
HONEY-ROASTED OR TOFFEE PEANUTS.

—PEANUT BUTTER SWIRL COFFEE CAKE—

TIME: 60 MINUTES   SERVES: 8–10

This combination of classic breakfast flavors melts in your mouth, and the added sweetness to the savory is incredible!

1 1/2 CUPS BUTTER, ROOM TEMPERATURE

1 1/2 CUPS SUGAR

3 EGGS, ROOM TEMPERATURE

1 1/2 TEASPOONS VANILLA EXTRACT

1 1/4 CUPS SOUR CREAM

2 1/2 CUPS ALL-PURPOSE FLOUR

2 TEASPOONS BAKING POWDER

1/2 TEASPOON SALT

1/2 CUP CHOPPED PEANUTS

FOR THE PEANUT BUTTER SWIRL:

1 TEASPOON CINNAMON

1/2 CUP BROWN SUGAR

1/4 CUP CREAMY PEANUT BUTTER

1 TABLESPOON BUTTER, SOFTENED

FOR THE GLAZE:

1 CUP POWDERED SUGAR

2 TABLESPOONS WHOLE MILK

1) Preheat oven to 350 degrees. Liberally coat the Bundt pan with butter or canola oil spray and lightly flour, tapping out the excess flour to create a thin, even coat.

2) In a stand mixer with a paddle attachment, cream together the butter and sugar until the mixture is light and fluffy. Once finished, add the eggs one at a time and beat until thoroughly incorporated, scraping down the sides of the bowl after each egg. Add the vanilla extract, followed by the sour cream.

3) In a separate, medium mixing bowl, combine flour, baking powder, and salt.

4) Add the flour mixture to the egg mixture and mix briefly—just enough to incorporate all ingredients.

5) Transfer mixture to the prepared Bundt pan and spread batter evenly throughout the pan.

6) For the peanut butter swirl, mix together the cinnamon, brown sugar, peanut butter, and butter in a small mixing bowl using a fork or whisk. Pour over the top of the cake batter.

7) Sprinkle the peanuts over the batter, then use a butter knife to swirl the streusel and peanuts into the cake batter.

8) Bake at 350 for 45-50 minutes or until a toothpick comes out mostly clean.

9) Allow the cake to rest in the pan for up to 30 minutes, then turn out of the pan and allow to completely cool on a wire cooling rack.

10) While the cake cools, whisk together the powdered sugar and milk to make the glaze. When the cake is mostly cool and has been turned out of the pan, use a whisk to drizzle the glaze over it.

—APPLE CIDER DOUGHNUT CAKE—

TIME: 70 MINUTES   SERVES: 8–10

Take those delicious apple cider doughnuts that you see at pumpkin patches and corn mazes in the fall, make them bigger, and you get this autumnal delight. This recipe uses a combination of whole wheat and all-purpose flour to give the cake a bit more texture and chew.

¾ CUP OLIVE OIL

1 ¾ CUPS SUGAR

3 EGGS, ROOM TEMPERATURE

2 TEASPOONS VANILLA EXTRACT

¾ CUP YOGURT

1 CUP APPLE CIDER

2 CUPS ALL-PURPOSE FLOUR

1 CUP WHOLE WHEAT FLOUR

1 ½ TEASPOON BAKING POWDER

1 ½ TEASPOON CINNAMON

½ TEASPOON BAKING SODA

¾ TEASPOON SALT

FOR THE CINNAMON SUGAR TOPPING:

¼ CUP SUGAR

1 TEASPOON CINNAMON

4 TABLESPOONS BUTTER, MELTED

1) Preheat the oven to 350 degrees. Liberally coat the Bundt pan with butter or canola oil spray and lightly flour, tapping out the excess flour to create a thin, even coat.

2) In a large mixing bowl, combine the olive oil and sugar. Whisk in one egg at a time. When the eggs are fully incorporated, add the vanilla extract, yogurt, and apple cider.

3) In a separate bowl, mix the all-purpose and whole wheat flours, baking powder, cinnamon, baking soda, and salt.

4) Add the flour mixture to the olive oil and sugar mixture, mixing just enough to incorporate each ingredient.

5) Transfer cake batter to the prepared Bundt pan. Bake at 350 for 45–50 minutes, or until a toothpick comes out mostly clean.

6) While the cake bakes, mix together the sugar and cinnamon for your cinnamon sugar topping.

7) When you've removed the cake from the oven, allow it to rest in the pan for up to 30 minutes, then turn out of the pan and allow to completely cool on a wire cooling rack.

8) As soon as the cake is turned out of the pan and still slightly warm, brush with melted butter then sprinkle the cinnamon sugar mixture over the cake until thoroughly coated.

—JELLY DOUGHNUT CAKE—

TIME: 90 MINUTES   SERVES: 8–10

Why buy a box of doughnuts when you could make one giant one to feed a crowd? This cake has all the flavor and fun of a doughnut shop treat, but you can customize it with your favorite jelly or flavors. For an authentic doughnut look, use a simpler Bundt pan over one with more decorative ridges.

³⁄₄ CUP OLIVE OIL

1 ³⁄₄ CUPS SUGAR

3 EGGS, ROOM TEMPERATURE

2 TEASPOONS VANILLA EXTRACT

³⁄₄ CUP YOGURT

1 CUP MILK

2 CUPS ALL-PURPOSE FLOUR

1 CUP WHOLE WHEAT FLOUR

1 ½ TEASPOON BAKING POWDER

1 ½ TEASPOON CINNAMON

½ TEASPOON BAKING SODA

³⁄₄ TEASPOON SALT

³⁄₄ CUP STRAWBERRY OR CHERRY JAM

POWDERED SUGAR, FOR DUSTING

1) Preheat the oven to 350 degrees. Liberally coat the Bundt pan with butter or canola oil spray and lightly flour, tapping out the excess flour to create a thin, even coat.

2) In a large mixing bowl, combine the olive oil and sugar. Whisk in one egg at a time. When the eggs are fully incorporated, add the vanilla extract, yogurt, and milk.

3) In a separate bowl, mix the all-purpose and whole wheat flours, baking powder, cinnamon, baking soda, and salt.

4) Add the flour mixture to the olive oil and sugar mixture, mixing just enough to incorporate each ingredient.

5) Transfer cake batter to the prepared Bundt pan. Bake at 350 for 45-50 minutes, or until a toothpick comes out mostly clean.

6) When you've removed the cake from the oven, allow it to rest in the pan for up to 30 minutes, then turn out of the pan and allow to completely cool on a wire cooling rack.

7) Once the cake has cooled completely, use a knife to slice the cake in half horizontally. Separate the two halves.

8) Spread the jelly over the bottom half of the cake. Replace the top half.

9) Sprinkle with powdered sugar before serving.

For Extra DECADENCE

ADD A LAYER OF WHIPPED CREAM OR BUTTERCREAM OVER THE JELLY.

—MINI BUNDT PAN DOUGHNUTS—

TIME: 30 MINUTES   SERVES: 10–12

Doughnuts are a favorite breakfast treat, and baking them in a mini Budnt pan not only makes them healthier than fried versions, but also adds adorable design. A mini Bundt pan is a perfect replacement for a traditional doughnut pan.

1 CUP ALL-PURPOSE FLOUR

1/2 TEASPOON BAKING POWDER

1/4 TEASPOON BAKING SODA

1/8 TEASPOON SALT

1/2 TEASPOON CINNAMON

1/4 CUP MILK

4 TABLESPOONS BUTTER, SOFTENED

1 EGG

1/2 CUP GRANULATED SUGAR

1 TEASPOON VANILLA EXTRACT

FOR THE TOPPING:

1 TEASPOON CINNAMON

1/2 CUP GRANULATED SUGAR

2 TABLESPOONS BUTTER, MELTED

1) Preheat the oven to 350 degrees. Prepare your mini Bundt pan by spraying with cooking spray or coating with butter. Be sure to thoroughly coat the pan to prevent sticking.

2) In a bowl, combine the flour, baking powder, baking soda, salt, and cinnamon.

3) In a separate bowl, beat the milk, butter, egg, sugar, and vanilla with a whisk or beater until smooth.

4) Pour the milk mixture into the flour mixture, stirring until just combined. Try not to overly mix the batter.

5) Using a spoon, pour the batter evenly into the mini Bundt molds. Do not fill the molds more than 2/3 of the way. Alternatively, the batter can be placed in a plastic bag with one corner cut, to be used as a piping bag to avoid dripping.

6) Bake the doughnuts for 10–12 minutes, or until lightly browned. Because the doughnuts are small, they will cook quickly, so start checking them early and use a toothpick to check whether they are done. When a toothpick comes cleanly from the center of a doughnut, they should be removed from the oven.

7) Prepare the topping while you allow the doughnuts to cool. In a bowl, combine the cinnamon and sugar.

8) When the doughnuts have cooled for about 10 minutes, but are still slightly warm, remove them from the pan. Brush the doughnuts with the melted butter, and coat them in the cinnamon and sugar topping.

—MINI BUNDT PAN CHOCOLATE DOUGHNUTS—

TIME: 30 MINUTES   SERVES: 10-12

Baking these classic chocolate doughnuts in a mini Bundt pan gives them a beautiful texture. For extra chocolate flavor, swap out the powdered sugar topping for a Chocolate Glaze (page 191).

1 CUP ALL-PURPOSE FLOUR

1/2 TEASPOON BAKING POWDER

1/4 TEASPOON BAKING SODA

1/8 TEASPOON SALT

3 TABLESPOONS COCOA POWDER

1/4 CUP MILK

4 TABLESPOONS BUTTER, SOFTENED

1 EGG

1/2 CUP GRANULATED SUGAR

1 TEASPOON VANILLA EXTRACT

POWDERED SUGAR, FOR DUSTING

1) Preheat the oven to 350 degrees. Prepare your mini Bundt pan by spraying with cooking spray or coating with butter. Be sure to thoroughly coat the pan to prevent sticking.

2) In a bowl, combine the flour, baking powder, baking soda, salt, and cocoa powder.

3) In a separate bowl, beat the milk, butter, egg, sugar, and vanilla with a whisk or beater until smooth.

4) Pour the milk mixture into the flour mixture, stirring until just combined. Try not to overly mix the batter.

5) Using a spoon, pour the batter evenly into the mini Bundt molds. Do not fill the molds more than ⅔ of the way. Alternatively, the batter can be placed in a plastic bag with one corner cut, to be used as a piping bag to avoid dripping.

6) Bake the doughnuts for 10-12 minutes, or until lightly browned. Because the doughnuts are small, they will cook quickly, so start checking them early and use a toothpick to check whether they are done. When a toothpick comes cleanly from the center of a doughnut, they should be removed from the oven.

7) When the doughnuts have cooled for about 10 minutes, but are still slightly warm, remove them from the pan. Dust the tops with powdered sugar.

—GLUTEN-FREE MINI BUNDT PAN—
PUMPKIN SPICE DOUGHNUTS

TIME: 35 MINUTES   SERVES: 10–12

There's nothing that tastes as much like autumn as the delicious combination of pumpkin spice. These doughnuts are best served slightly warm, and are delicious with a Vanilla Glaze (page 188) or a Cream Cheese Glaze (page 191). And the best part is that this recipe is gluten-free!

1 CUP GLUTEN-FREE FLOUR

½ TEASPOON XANTHAN GUM

1 TEASPOON CINNAMON

½ TEASPOON NUTMEG

¼ TEASPOON ALLSPICE

⅛ TEASPOON SALT

½ TEASPOON BAKING POWDER

¼ TEASPOON BAKING SODA

1 CUP PUMPKIN PUREE

4 TABLESPOONS BUTTER, MELTED

1 EGG

½ CUP GRANULATED SUGAR

1 TEASPOON VANILLA EXTRACT

1) Preheat the oven to 350 degrees. Prepare your mini Bundt pan by spraying with cooking spray or coating with butter. Be sure to thoroughly coat the pan to prevent sticking.

2) In a bowl, combine the gluten-free flour, xanthan gum, cinnamon, nutmeg, allspice, salt, baking powder, and baking soda.

3) In a separate bowl, beat the pumpkin, butter, egg, sugar, and vanilla with a whisk or beater until smooth.

4) Pour the milk mixture into the flour mixture, stirring until just combined. Try not to overly mix the batter.

5) Using a spoon, pour the batter evenly into the mini Bundt molds. Do not fill the molds more than ⅔ of the way. Alternatively, the batter can be placed in a plastic bag with one corner cut, to be used as a piping bag to avoid dripping.

6) Bake the doughnuts for 10–12 minutes, or until lightly browned. Because the doughnuts are small, they will cook quickly, so start checking them early and use a toothpick to check whether they are done. When a toothpick comes cleanly from the center of a doughnut, they should be removed from the oven.

7) Prepare the topping while you allow the doughnuts to cool. In a bowl, combine the cinnamon and sugar.

8) When the doughnuts have cooled for about 10 minutes, but are still slightly warm, remove them from the pan.

If you'd prefer to use regular flour, swap the gluten-free blend for 1 cup all-purpose flour and omit the xanthan gum.

—LEMON POPPYSEED MUFFIN CAKE—

TIME: 60 MINUTES   SERVES: 8–10

Meet your new go-to summer picnic treat. Or your new favorite breakfast cake. Whether pairing it with rosé or coffee, you can't go wrong with this tasty citrus confection. For a more dessert flavor, add a Lemon Glaze (page 196).

1 CUP BUTTER, ROOM TEMPERATURE

2 CUPS SUGAR

4 EGGS, ROOM TEMPERATURE

1 TEASPOON VANILLA EXTRACT

1/2 CUP FRESH LEMON JUICE

1 CUP PLAIN GREEK YOGURT

2 3/4 CUPS ALL-PURPOSE FLOUR

3/4 TEASPOON SALT

1/2 TEASPOON BAKING SODA

1 TEASPOON BAKING POWDER

4 TABLESPOONS POPPY SEEDS

1) Preheat oven to 350 degrees. Liberally coat the Bundt pan with butter or canola oil spray and lightly flour, tapping out the excess flour to create a thin, even coat.

2) In a stand mixer with a paddle attachment, cream together the butter and sugar until the mixture is light and fluffy. Once finished, add the eggs one at a time and beat until thoroughly incorporated, scraping down the sides of the bowl after each egg.

3) Add vanilla extract, lemon juice and Greek yogurt to the egg mixture. Once incorporated, scrape down the sides of the bowl using a rubber spatula.

4) In a separate medium mixing bowl, combine flour, salt, baking soda, baking powder and poppy seeds.

5) Add the flour mixture to the wet mixture, mixing just enough to incorporate. Scrape the bowl with the rubber spatula to ensure full integration.

6) Transfer the mixture to your prepared Bundt pan and spread batter evenly throughout the pan. Bake at 350 for 45–50 minutes, or until a toothpick comes out mostly clean.

7) Remove from heat and let the cake to rest in the pan for up to 30 minutes, then turn out of the pan and allow to completely cool on a wire cooling rack.

—BLUEBERRY MUFFIN CAKE—

TIME: 60 MINUTES   SERVES: 8–10

Want the muffins without the wrappers?
This classic breakfast food is so easy to slice up and serve a crowd.

1 CUP BUTTER, ROOM
TEMPERATURE

2 CUPS SUGAR

4 EGGS, ROOM
TEMPERATURE

1 TEASPOON VANILLA
EXTRACT

1/2 CUP FRESH LEMON JUICE

1 CUP PLAIN GREEK YOGURT

2 3/4 CUPS ALL-PURPOSE
FLOUR

3/4 TEASPOON SALT

1/2 TEASPOON BAKING SODA

1 TEASPOON BAKING
POWDER

3/4 CUP FRESH BLUEBERRIES

1) Preheat oven to 350 degrees. Liberally coat the Bundt pan with butter or canola oil spray and lightly flour, tapping out the excess flour to create a thin, even coat.

2) In a stand mixer with a paddle attachment, cream together the butter and sugar until the mixture is light and fluffy. Once finished, add the eggs one at a time and beat until thoroughly incorporated, scraping down the sides of the bowl after each egg.

3) Add vanilla extract, lemon juice and Greek yogurt to the egg mixture. Once incorporated, scrape down the sides of the bowl using a rubber spatula.

4) In a separate medium mixing bowl, combine flour, salt, baking soda, baking powder and blueberries.

5) Add the flour mixture to the wet mixture, mixing just enough to incorporate. Scrape the bowl with the rubber spatula to ensure full integration.

6) Transfer the mixture to your prepared Bundt pan and spread batter evenly throughout the pan. Bake at 350 for 45-50 minutes, or until a toothpick comes out mostly clean.

7) Remove from heat and let the cake to rest in the pan for up to 30 minutes, then turn out of the pan and allow to completely cool on a wire cooling rack.

—VEGETABLE FRITTATA—

TIME: 60 MINUTES   SERVES: 4–6

This frittata will get a little messy, and that's a good thing. If you don't want to risk turning it out of the pan, don't sweat it—the Bundt doubles as a gorgeous serving dish.

1 TABLESPOON OLIVE OIL

1 PINT MUSHROOMS, SLICED

1-2 WHITE STALKS OF LEEK, DICED AND CLEANED WELL

4 OUNCES SOFT GOAT CHEESE, PINCHED INTO SMALL HALF-BITE-SIZED PIECES

8 EGGS

2 TABLESPOONS MILK

SALT AND PEPPER, TO TASTE

1) Preheat oven to 350 degrees and grease the Bundt pan with canola oil spray.

2) In a large skillet, heat 1 tablespoon of olive oil over medium heat and sauté the leeks until they're translucent and fragrant, about 3 minutes. Add mushrooms to skillet and sauté for another 2 minutes. Transfer the leeks and mushrooms to the prepared Bundt pan, spreading evenly.

3) In a medium mixing bowl, whisk together eggs, milk, salt, pepper and goat cheese. Pour the mixture over contents of the Bundt pan.

4) Cook for 30–35 minutes, until the eggs appear to be set but not dry. A little jiggle is good; a little wetness is even better. Let cool for 5 minutes before turning the frittata onto a plate to serve.

—FRENCH TOAST—

TIME: 60 MINUTES   SERVES: 8

A breakfast staple, French Toast is made even more delicious by baking it in a gooey, pull-apart ring. After removing the bread from the pan, drizzle the whole loaf with maple syrup.

2 CUPS HALF AND HALF OR MILK

4 EGGS

1 TABLESPOON VANILLA EXTRACT

1/2 TEASPOON CINNAMON

PINCH OF NUTMEG

1 LOAF BRIOCHE BREAD, CUT INTO 1-INCH CUBES

1 TABLESPOON BUTTER, MELTED, FOR SERVING

MAPLE SYRUP, FOR SERVING

1) Preheat the oven to 350 degrees and grease your Bundt pan with butter or cooking spray.

2) In a bowl, combine the half and half, eggs, vanilla, cinnamon, and nutmeg with a whisk or fork.

3) Add the cubes of bread to the egg mixture and combine. Allow the mixture to sit for about 5 minutes.

4) Remove the bread from the egg mixture and place it in the Bundt pan.

5) Bake for 40-45 minutes, or until the bread is golden brown.

6) Allow the bread to cool for 5-10 minutes.

7) Remove the bread from the Bundt pan and drizzle with melted butter and maple syrup before serving.

For Extra **SWEETNESS**

ADD 1 CUP FRESH, SLICED STRAWBERRIES OR 1 CUP FRESH BLUEBERRIES WHEN YOU COMBINE THE BREAD AND EGG MIXTURE.

—HONEY OATMEAL BUNDT CAKE—

TIME: 70 MINUTES   SERVES: 8

Add excitement to your morning oatmeal by baking it into a delicious breakfast cake.
A piece of this sweet cake is much more enticing than a boring granola bar!

2 CUPS ALL-PURPOSE FLOUR

1 TEASPOON BAKING POWDER

1/2 TEASPOON BAKING SODA

1 TEASPOON CINNAMON

1/2 CUP BUTTER, ROOM TEMPERATURE

1/2 CUP GRANULATED SUGAR

1/2 CUP PACKED BROWN SUGAR

3 EGGS

1/2 CUP HONEY

1/2 CUP MILK

1 TEASPOON VANILLA EXTRACT

1 CUP ROLLED OATS

1) Preheat the oven to 350 degrees. Prepare your Bundt pan by greasing thoroughly with butter or cooking spray.

2) In a bowl, combine the flour, baking soda, baking powder, and cinnamon. Set the bowl aside.

3) Using a beater or stand mixture, beat the butter on medium speed until smooth. Add the granulated and brown sugar, and beat until combined. Add the eggs, one at a time, and beat until combined. Add the honey, and beat until combined.

4) Pour the flour mixture into the egg mixture, and mix until just combined. Add the milk and vanilla, and mix slowly until just combined.

5) Pour the batter into the prepared Bundt pan. Sprinkle the oats over the top of the batter.

6) Bake for 45-50 minutes, or until a toothpick inserted into the center comes out clean.

7) Allow the cake to cool for 20 minutes before removing from the pan.

—APPLESAUCE OATMEAL BUNDT CAKE—

TIME: 70 MINUTES   SERVES: 8

This delicious applesauce cake is great as a breakfast snack, but adding a Caramel Glaze (page 199) and chopped walnuts to the top turns this basic into a showstopping dessert.

2 CUPS ALL-PURPOSE FLOUR

1 TEASPOON BAKING POWDER

1/2 TEASPOON BAKING SODA

1 TEASPOON CINNAMON

1/2 CUP BUTTER, ROOM TEMPERATURE

1/2 CUP GRANULATED SUGAR

1/2 CUP PACKED BROWN SUGAR

3 EGGS

1 CUP APPLESAUCE

1 TEASPOON VANILLA EXTRACT

1 CUP ROLLED OATS

1/2 CUP WALNUTS, CHOPPED

CARAMEL GLAZE (PAGE 199), IF DESIRED

1) Preheat the oven to 350 degrees. Prepare your Bundt pan by greasing thoroughly with butter or cooking spray.

2) In a bowl, combine the flour, baking soda, baking powder, and cinnamon. Set the bowl aside.

3) Using a beater or stand mixture, beat the butter on medium speed until smooth. Add the granulated and brown sugar, and beat until combined. Add the eggs, one at a time, and beat until combined. Add the honey, and beat until combined.

4) Pour the flour mixture into the egg mixture, and mix until just combined. Add the milk and vanilla, and mix slowly until just combined.

5) Add the oats and walnuts, reserving some for topping if desired, to the batter, and mix until just combined.

6) Pour the batter into the prepared Bundt pan.

7) Bake for 45-50 minutes, or until a toothpick inserted into the center comes out clean.

8) Allow the cake to cool for 20 minutes before removing from the pan.

9) Top with Caramel Glaze (page 199) and remaining walnuts, if desired.

Innovative Ideas:

SIMPLE CENTERPIECE

With its center hole, the Bundt cake is primed to be the perfect centerpiece for any table. A simple candle or bunch of flowers perfectly fit in the middle, and turn this cake into a decoration to put on your table for beauty during dinner and a sweet treat for dessert.

DRINK COOLER

Instead of a dirty bucket you hastily clean out before guests arrive, use one of your beautiful Bundts to serve drinks. Just fill it with ice, add the drinks then serve. The pans higher walls help the drinks stand straighter than they would in a regular bowl, and the pan's tasteful design will match a dinner party's décor better than a cooler or bucket.

ICE RING

There are dinner parties, and then there are dinner *parties*. If you're shooting for the latter, why not give your punch bowl some extra decoration with a beautiful Bundt-shaped ice sculpture? Not only will its appearance dazzle guests—the solid block of ice will melt more slowly, avoiding that unpleasant watered-down punch everybody avoids after an hour or so.

Breads

Bread making doesn't have to be tedious. In fact, the Bundt pan makes absolutely perfect bread for a crowd. By shaping small sections of dough in the Bundt ring, breads become delicious pull-apart breads. Consider adding a bowl of frosting or dip to the center (page 124) for a decorative touch.

—MONKEY BREAD—

If you're concerned about your level of fanciness, feel free to make a brioche recipe and proceed with chilled brioche in place of refrigerated biscuits.

½ CUP BROWN SUGAR

1 CUP SUGAR

½ TEASPOON SALT

1 CUP BUTTER

1 TABLESPOON CINNAMON

3 CANS REFRIGERATED BUTTERMILK BISCUITS

½ CUP PECANS, CHOPPED

1) Preheat the oven to 350 degrees. Liberally coat the Bundt pan with butter or canola oil spray.

2) In a medium saucepan, melt the butter, brown sugar, white sugar, salt and cinnamon just until they've combined, then set aside to cool slightly.

3) Remove all 3 cans of biscuit dough from their containers and slice each biscuit into quarters. Place the dough pieces into one large mixing bowl. Pour the butter mixture over the dough pieces and mix well using your hands. Add the pecans and combine.

4) Place the sugarcoated dough pieces into your prepared Bundt pan. Pour any remaining butter mixture over the dough in the pan.

5) Bake for 35-40 minutes or until the dough at the top of the pan looks golden and crisp. Serve warm.

−BLUEBERRY CINNAMON MONKEY BREAD−

TIME: 50 MINUTES   SERVES: 10–12

The fresh taste of blueberry is a perfect pairing for this sticky treat. Don't be afraid to get your hands a little messy!

1/2 CUP BROWN SUGAR

1 CUP SUGAR

1/2 TEASPOON SALT

1 CUP BUTTER

1 TABLESPOON CINNAMON

3 CANS REFRIGERATED BUTTERMILK BISCUITS

1 CUP FRESH BLUEBERRIES

1) Preheat the oven to 350 degrees. Liberally coat the Bundt pan with butter or canola oil spray.

2) In a medium saucepan, melt the butter, brown sugar, white sugar, salt and cinnamon just until they've combined, then set aside to cool slightly.

3) Remove all 3 cans of biscuit dough from their containers and slice each biscuit into quarters. Place the dough pieces into one large mixing bowl. Pour the butter mixture over the dough pieces and mix well using your hands.

4) Add the blueberries to the mixture and combine.

5) Place the sugarcoated dough pieces into your prepared Bundt pan. Pour any remaining butter mixture over the dough in the pan.

6) Bake for 35–40 minutes or until the dough at the top of the pan looks golden and crisp. Serve warm.

—CRANBERRY ORANGE MONKEY BREAD—

TIME: 50 MINUTES   **SERVES: 10–12**

Cranberry and orange is a fantastic flavor combination, and this new and improved recipe is sure to impress!

1 ½ CUPS GRANULATED SUGAR

½ TEASPOON SALT

½ CUP BUTTER

½ CUP ORANGE JUICE

1 CUP CRANBERRIES, HALVED

3 CANS REFRIGERATED BUTTERMILK BISCUITS

1) Preheat the oven to 350 degrees. Liberally coat the Bundt pan with butter or canola oil spray.

2) In a medium saucepan, melt the butter, white sugar, and salt just until they've combined. Remove from the heat, and add the orange juice and cranberries. Combine, and then set aside to cool slightly.

3) Remove all 3 cans of biscuit dough from their containers and slice each biscuit into quarters. Place the dough pieces into one large mixing bowl. Pour the butter mixture over the dough pieces and mix well using your hands.

4) Place the sugarcoated dough pieces into your prepared Bundt pan. Pour any remaining butter mixture over the dough in the pan.

5) Bake for 35-40 minutes or until the dough at the top of the pan looks golden and crisp. Serve warm.

—CINNAMON SUGAR MONKEY BREAD—

TIME: 50 MINUTES   SERVES: 10–12

This sweet monkey bread is absolutely irresistible. Be prepared to make multiple batches of this one!

1 ½ CUPS SUGAR

1 TABLESPOON CINNAMON

½ CUP BUTTER, MELTED

3 CANS REFRIGERATED BUTTERMILK BISCUITS

1) Preheat the oven to 350 degrees. Liberally coat the Bundt pan with butter or canola oil spray.

2) In a bowl, combine the cinnamon and sugar.

3) Remove all 3 cans of biscuit dough from their containers and slice each biscuit into quarters. Place the dough pieces into a large mixing bowl. Pour the butter over the dough pieces and mix well using your hands.

4) Add the cinnamon and sugar mixture to the bread and combine, until each piece is well coated with sugar.

5) Place the sugarcoated dough pieces into your prepared Bundt pan. Pour any remaining butter mixture over the dough in the pan.

6) Bake for 35-40 minutes or until the dough at the top of the pan looks golden and crisp. Serve warm.

−DINNER ROLLS−

TIME: 3 HOURS   SERVES: 12

These classic dinner rolls are light, flaky, and buttery perfection.

1 ¼ CUPS WHOLE MILK, HEATED TO 110 DEGREES

3 TABLESPOONS SUGAR

1 TABLESPOON ACTIVE DRY YEAST

8 TABLESPOONS (1 STICK) UNSALTED BUTTER

¾ TEASPOON SALT

2 EGGS AT ROOM TEMPERATURE, LIGHTLY BEATEN

3 ½ CUPS CAKE OR BREAD FLOUR (NOT ALL-PURPOSE FLOUR)

1) In a small bowl, combine ½ cup warm milk and the sugar. Sprinkle the yeast over it, stir, and set aside so the yeast can proof (about 10 minutes).

2) While the yeast is proofing, melt the butter in a skillet over low to medium heat, and remove from heat when melted.

3) When the yeast mix is frothy, stir in 3 tablespoons of the melted butter, the remaining milk, the salt, and the eggs. Then stir in the flour, mixing until all ingredients are incorporated. Transfer to a lightly floured surface and knead the dough for 5 to 10 minutes until it is soft and springy and elastic.

4) Coat the bottom and sides of a large mixing bowl (ceramic is best) with butter.

5) Place the ball of dough in the bowl, cover loosely with plastic wrap, put it in a naturally warm, draft-free location, and let it rise until doubled in size, about 45 minutes to 1 hour.

6) Prepare a lightly floured surface to work on. Punch down the dough in the bowl and transfer it to the floured surface.

7) If the remaining melted butter has started to re-solidify, reheat.

8) Break off pieces of the dough to form into rolls, shaping them into 2-inch balls with your hands. Roll the balls in the melted butter, and place them in the bottom of the Bundt pan.

9) Cover the Bundt loosely with a clean dish towel, put it in the warm, draftfree spot, and let the rolls rise until doubled in size, about 30 minutes. While they're rising, preheat the oven to 350 degrees.

10) When the rolls have risen and the oven is ready, cover the Bundt with aluminum foil and bake in the oven for 20 minutes. Remove the foil and finish cooking, another 15 minutes or so, until the rolls are golden on top and light and springy. Serve warm.

—PEPPERONI BREAD—

TIME: 3 HOURS   SERVES: 6–8

This is a favorite during football season, when the game hasn't actually started until this makes an appearance in front of the TV. Start in the morning for an afternoon game, as the dough needs to rise several times. But it's so delicious!

1¼ CUPS WATER (110 TO 115 DEGREES)

1 OUNCE ACTIVE DRY YEAST

1 TABLESPOON SUGAR

1 TABLESPOON MELTED BUTTER

1 ½ TEASPOONS SALT

3½ CUPS FLOUR

SALT AND PEPPER

½ POUND PEPPERONI, SLIVERED

2 CUPS GRATED MOZZARELLA CHEESE

1 TEASPOON HOT PEPPER FLAKES

1 TEASPOON DRIED OREGANO

1 TEASPOON GARLIC POWDER

1) 1. Proof the yeast by mixing the water and sugar in a large bowl and then adding the yeast, stirring. Let sit until foamy, about 10 minutes. Add the salt and about half the flour to form a sticky dough. Cover the bowl with plastic wrap or a clean dish towel and let rise in a warm, draft-free place until it is double in size, about 1 hour.

2) 2. Punch down the dough and add more flour to make it less sticky. Transfer to a floured surface and work the dough until it's smooth and elastic. Transfer to a lightly greased bowl and let sit for about 15 minutes.

3) 3. On the floured surface, roll the dough out into a rectangle about 14 x 16 inches. Sprinkle with salt and pepper, spread the dough with pieces of pepperoni, then cheese, and top with a sprinkling of hot pepper flakes, oregano, and garlic powder. Roll up like a jellyroll, pinching the ends to secure filling.

4) 4. Grease the Bundt with the butter and lay the roll in it in a circle, working in a spiral. Cover with a clean dish towel and let it rise again for about 1 hour. Preheat the oven to 375 degrees.

5) 5. Bake the pepperoni bread for about 30 minutes, until golden on top and bubbling in the center. Serve immediately.

Proof YOUR YEAST

IT'S IMPORTANT TO PROOF THE YEAST BEFORE ADDING IT TO YOUR RECIPE TO ENSURE THAT IT IS FRESH AND ACTIVE. IF IT IS, IT REACTS WITH THE SUGAR AND LIQUID AND CREATES TINY BUBBLES.

—HERB PULL-APART BREAD—

This delicious herb bread makes the perfect centerpiece to any meal. The aroma of the fresh herbs will have every guest reaching for a piece.

5 TABLESPOONS BUTTER

2 TABLESPOONS FRESH THYME, FINELY CHOPPED

1 TABLESPOON FRESH ROSEMARY, FINELY CHOPPED

2 TABLESPOON HALF AND HALF

1 ½ TEASPOONS SALT

FRESH GROUND BLACK PEPPER

2 LARGE CAN REFRIGERATED BISCUITS

2 TABLESPOONS FRESH CHIVES, FINELY CHOPPED

1) Preheat oven to 350 degrees. In a small saucepan under medium-low heat, melt the butter. Remove from the heat and pour into a small bowl. Add the thyme, rosemary, half and half, salt and black pepper to taste, and stir. If the mixture does not come together perfectly, don't panic—that's perfectly fine.

2) Open the cans of biscuits. Cut each biscuit into 4 pieces and add to a large bowl. Pour the butter mixture over the biscuit pieces and toss until evenly coated.

3) Grease the Bundt pan and arrange the biscuit pieces inside, being careful not to pack the pieces tightly as they will expand upon cooking. Bake for 30-40 minutes or until golden brown and crispy.

4) Remove from oven and move to a plate to cool for 5 minutes. Garnish with chives and serve.

—CHEESY GARLIC PULL-APART BREAD—

TIME: 45 MINUTES   SERVES: 15

Homemade cheesy bread? Enough said. This one is sure to stop traffic at any dinner party—be prepared to make more than one batch.

3 TABLESPOONS BUTTER, MELTED

1 TABLESPOON OLIVE OIL

3 CLOVES GARLIC, MINCED

2 TABLESPOONS PARSLEY

FRESH GROUND BLACK PEPPER

1 1/2 TEASPOONS SALT

2 LARGE CAN REFRIGERATED BISCUITS

1/2 CUP CHOPPED PARSLEY

1 1/2 CUPS SHREDDED CHEDDAR CHEESE

1) Preheat oven to 350 degrees. In a small saucepan under medium-low heat, melt the butter.

2) In a bowl, combine the melted butter, olive oil, garlic, parsley, salt, and pepper.

3) Open the cans of biscuits. Cut each biscuit into 4 pieces and add to a large bowl. Pour the butter mixture over the biscuit pieces and toss until evenly coated.

4) Grease the Bundt pan and arrange the biscuit pieces inside, being careful not to pack the pieces tightly as they will expand upon cooking. Bake for 25 minutes or until golden brown and crispy.

5) Remove from the oven and let cool for 5 minutes. Using a potholder or kitchen towel, turn the hot bread out onto a baking sheet and cover with shredded cheese. Return to the oven for 5-10 minutes or until cheese is melted. Remove from oven and move to a plate to cool for 5 minutes.

There's no such thing **AS TOO MUCH CHEESE!**

TRY ADDING PARMESAN OR MOZZARELLA FOR AN EXTRA BLAST CHEESY GOODNESS.

—CHEDDAR RANCH PULL-APART BREAD—

TIME: 45 MINUTES   SERVES: 15

Cheddar and ranch is an incredible flavor combination, and your guests won't be able to get enough of this pull-apart bread. For an extra blast of ranch flavor, pour some ranch dressing in a small bowl and place it in the center hole.

5 TABLESPOONS BUTTER

2 TABLESPOON HALF AND HALF

FRESH GROUND BLACK PEPPER

1 ½ TEASPOONS SALT

1 PACKET RANCH SEASONING

2 LARGE CAN REFRIGERATED BISCUITS

1 CUP SHREDDED CHEDDAR CHEESE

1) Preheat oven to 350 degrees.

2) In a bowl, combine the melted butter, half and half, salt, black pepper to taste, and ranch seasoning packet, and stir. If the mixture does not come together perfectly, don't panic—that's perfectly fine.

3) Open the cans of biscuits. Cut each biscuit into 4 pieces and add to a large bowl. Pour the butter mixture over the biscuit pieces and toss until evenly coated.

4) Grease the Bundt pan and arrange the biscuit pieces inside, being careful not to pack the pieces tightly as they will expand upon cooking. Bake for 25 minutes or until golden brown and crispy.

5) Remove from the oven and let cool for 5 minutes. Using a potholder or kitchen towel, turn the hot bread out onto a baking sheet and cover with shredded cheese. Return to the oven for 5-10 minutes or until cheese is melted. Remove from oven and move to a plate to cool for 5 minutes.

—SWIRLED CINNAMON BREAD—

TIME: 3 HOURS MINUTES   SERVES: 8–10

There is no better smell than freshly baked bread, and using a Bundt pan for this loaf is sure to make it a crowd-pleaser. Unlike other swirled breads, this recipe incorporates the cinnamon directly into the dough to avoid the bread separating from the layer of cinnamon.

1/2 OUNCE ACTIVE DRY YEAST

3/4 CUP WATER (110 TO 115 DEGREES)

1/2 CUP MILK

6 TABLESPOONS BUTTER, SOFTENED

2 EGGS

1/2 CUP SUGAR, PLUS 1 TABLESPOON

1 TEASPOON SALT

6 CUPS ALL-PURPOSE FLOUR

2 TABLESPOONS CINNAMON

2 TABLESPOONS BROWN SUGAR

1) In a large bowl, combine the water and 1 tablespoon of sugar. Add the yeast and stir to dissolve, then allow the yeast to proof for about 10 minutes.

2) Add the milk, butter, eggs, sugar, and salt to the proofed yeast. Whisk until smooth.

3) Slowly stir in the flour to form a soft dough. Split the dough in half to form two balls.

4) To one of the dough balls, add the cinnamon and brown sugar. Mix until just combined.

5) On a floured surface, kneed the dough balls for about 8-10 minutes. Grease two bowls with butter, and place one dough ball in each bowl. Cover the bowls with plastic wrap or a clean dish towel and let rise in a warm, draft-free place until the dough is double in size, about 1 hour.

6) Thoroughly grease your Bundt pan with butter or canola oil spray.

7) Prepare a lightly floured surface to work on. Punch down the dough in the bowls and transfer them to the floured surface.

8) Stretch one ball of dough into a roughly 12 x 15 inch rectangle. Repeat with the second ball of dough. Place the cinnamon rectangle on top of the plain dough rectangle.

9) Starting at the short end of the rectangle, lightly roll the dough into a log. Be careful not to roll too tightly. Place the dough in the Bundt pan, overlapping at the ends if necessary.

10) Tent the pan with aluminum foil or plastic wrap and allow the dough to rise for about 30 minutes in a warm, draft-free place.

11) Preheat the oven to 375 degrees.

12) Bake the bread for about 40-45 minutes, or until the crust is golden brown and firm to the touch.

13) Loosen the edges of the bread with a spatula or knife, and allow it to cool for about 15 minutes before removing from the pan.

—CORNBREAD—

Brace yourselves for a savory nirvana. This is the perfect side for any meal, but try it with a comfort food staple like meatloaf for an extra rich meal that's sure to leave you satisfied—and maybe a little sleepy.

1 ½ CUP MEDIUM-GRIND CORNMEAL

½ CUP ALL-PURPOSE FLOUR

1 ½ TEASPOONS BAKING POWDER

1 TEASPOON SALT

¼ CUP SUGAR

4 TABLESPOONS BUTTER, MELTED

2 EGGS

1 ¼ CUP MILK

1) Preheat the oven to 375 degrees. Prepare the Bundt pan with butter or canola oil spray and coat with a thin layer of flour, tapping out the excess flour to create a thin, even coat.

2) In a large mixing bowl, combine the cornmeal, flour, baking powder, salt and sugar.

3) In a small mixing bowl, combine the cooled melted butter, eggs, and milk. Add the wet ingredients to the dry ingredients and mix well.

4) Transfer the batter to the prepared Bundt pan and bake for 40–45 minutes or until a toothpick comes out mostly clean. Remove from the oven and let cool for 10 minutes before turning out of the pan.

—JALAPEÑO CHEDDAR CORNBREAD—

TIME: 40 MINUTES   SERVES: 6–8

Add a little southern spice to basic cornbread with jalapeño and cheddar cheese. This savory combination is sure to surprise your tastebuds. If you like a little extra heat, leave some of the jalapeño seeds in—they're the spiciest part of the pepper!

1 ½ CUP MEDIUM-GRIND CORNMEAL

½ CUP ALL-PURPOSE FLOUR

1 ½ TEASPOONS BAKING POWDER

1 TEASPOON SALT

¼ CUP SUGAR

4 TABLESPOONS BUTTER, MELTED

2 EGGS

1 ¼ CUP MILK

2 JALAPEÑOS, SEEDED AND DICED

½ CUP CHEDDAR CHEESE

1) Preheat the oven to 375 degrees. Prepare the Bundt pan with butter or canola oil spray and coat with a thin layer of flour, tapping out the excess flour to create a thin, even coat.

2) In a large mixing bowl, combine the cornmeal, flour, baking powder, salt and sugar.

3) In a small mixing bowl, combine the cooled melted butter, eggs, and milk. Add the wet ingredients to the dry ingredients and mix well.

4) Add the jalapeños and cheese to the cornbread batter and mix until just combined.

5) Transfer the batter to the prepared Bundt pan and bake for 40-45 minutes or until a toothpick comes out mostly clean. Remove from the oven and let cool for 10 minutes before turning out of the pan.

—GLUTEN-FREE CORNBREAD—

TIME: 40 MINUTES   SERVES: 6–8

Nobody should be left out of the cornbread fun, and this gluten-free version is sure to satisfy everyone. A little honey and some extra cornmeal replaces the flour naturally. This bread might not have exactly the same fluffy texture of bread with flour, but the sweet taste more than makes up for it!

2 CUP MEDIUM-GRIND CORNMEAL

1 1/2 TEASPOONS BAKING POWDER

1 TEASPOON SALT

1/4 CUP SUGAR

4 TABLESPOONS BUTTER, MELTED

2 EGGS

1 1/4 CUP MILK

1/4 CUP HONEY

1) Preheat the oven to 375 degrees. Prepare the Bundt pan with butter or canola oil spray and coat with a thin layer of flour, tapping out the excess flour to create a thin, even coat.

2) In a large mixing bowl, combine the cornmeal, baking powder, salt and sugar.

3) In a small mixing bowl, combine the cooled melted butter, eggs, milk, and honey. Add the wet ingredients to the dry ingredients and mix well.

4) Transfer the batter to the prepared Bundt pan and bake for 40-45 minutes or until a toothpick comes out mostly clean. Remove from the oven and let cool for 10 minutes before turning out of the pan.

—ZUCCHINI BREAD—

TIME: 70 MINUTES   SERVES: 8–10

Zucchini is a hearty ingredient for a bread, and baking this loaf in a Bundt pan gives interesting texture to an interesting flavor combination.

3 TABLESPOONS BUTTER, MELTED

1 CUP WHITE SUGAR

1 CUP BROWN SUGAR

½ CUP VEGETABLE OIL

1 TEASPOON VANILLA EXTRACT

2 EGGS, BEATEN

2 CUPS GRATED ZUCCHINI

3 CUPS ALL-PURPOSE FLOUR

1 TEASPOON BAKING SODA

1 TEASPOON BAKING POWDER

1 TEASPOON CINNAMON

½ TEASPOON GROUND NUTMEG

½ TEASPOON SALT

1) Preheat oven to 350 degrees. Liberally coat the Bundt pan with butter or canola oil spray and lightly flour, tapping out the excess flour to create a thin, even coat.

2) In a stand mixer with a paddle attachment, cream together the butter, white sugar, brown sugar, vegetable oil, and vanilla until the mixture is light and fluffy. Once finished, add the eggs one at a time and beat until thoroughly incorporated, scraping down the sides of the bowl after each egg. Add the zucchini, and stir briefly to combine.

3) In a separate medium mixing bowl, combine the flour, baking soda, baking powder, cinnamon, nutmeg, and salt. Add flour mixture to butter-sugar mixture and mix briefly—just until ingredients have been incorporated.

4) Transfer mixture to the prepared Bundt pan and spread batter evenly throughout the pan. Bake at 350 for 45–50 minutes, or until a toothpick comes out mostly clean.

5) Let the cake rest for 30 minutes, then turn out of the pan and allow to completely cool on a wire cooling rack.

—PARMESAN ZUCCHINI BREAD—

TIME: 70 MINUTES   SERVES: 8–10

This variation on cheesy bread has the healthy vegetable twist of zucchini added to it.

3 TABLESPOONS BUTTER, MELTED

1/2 CUP VEGETABLE OIL

1/4 CUP MILK

2 EGGS, BEATEN

2 CUPS GRATED ZUCCHINI

2 CUPS ALL-PURPOSE FLOUR

1 TEASPOON BAKING SODA

1 TEASPOON BAKING POWDER

1/2 TEASPOON GARLIC POWDER

1/2 TEASPOON ONION POWDER

1/2 TEASPOON SALT

3/4 CUP GRATED PARMESAN CHEESE

1/2 CUP SHREDDED CHEDDAR CHEESE

1) Preheat oven to 350 degrees. Liberally coat the Bundt pan with butter or canola oil spray and lightly flour, tapping out the excess flour to create a thin, even coat.

2) In a stand mixer with a paddle attachment, cream together the butter, milk, and vegetable oil. Add the eggs one at a time and beat until thoroughly incorporated, scraping down the sides of the bowl after each egg. Add the zucchini, and stir briefly to combine.

3) In a separate medium mixing bowl, combine the flour, baking soda, baking powder, garlic powder, onion powder, and salt. Add flour mixture to butter mixture and mix briefly—just until ingredients have been incorporated.

4) Add the Parmesan and cheddar cheese and mix until just combined.

5) Transfer mixture to the prepared Bundt pan and spread batter evenly throughout the pan. Bake at 350 for 45-50 minutes, or until a toothpick comes out mostly clean.

6) Let the cake rest for 30 minutes, then turn out of the pan and allow to completely cool on a wire cooling rack.

—CRANBERRY WALNUT ZUCCHINI BREAD—

TIME: 70 MINUTES   SERVES: 8–10

This delicious take on zucchini bread packs an extra punch. The tart bite of the cranberries and the crunch of the walnuts is the perfect combination for a tasty bread. Try a slice for breakfast to start your day off on the right foot!

3 TABLESPOONS BUTTER, MELTED

1 CUP WHITE SUGAR

1 CUP BROWN SUGAR

1/2 CUP VEGETABLE OIL

1 TEASPOON VANILLA EXTRACT

2 EGGS, BEATEN

2 CUPS GRATED ZUCCHINI

3 CUPS ALL-PURPOSE FLOUR

1 TEASPOON BAKING SODA

1 TEASPOON BAKING POWDER

1 TEASPOON CINNAMON

1/2 TEASPOON GROUND NUTMEG

1/2 TEASPOON SALT

3/4 CUP CRANBERRIES, HALVED

3/4 CUP WALNUTS, CHOPPED

1) Preheat oven to 350 degrees. Liberally coat the Bundt pan with butter or canola oil spray and lightly flour, tapping out the excess flour to create a thin, even coat.

2) In a stand mixer with a paddle attachment, cream together the butter, white sugar, brown sugar, vegetable oil, and vanilla until the mixture is light and fluffy. Once finished, add the eggs one at a time and beat until thoroughly incorporated, scraping down the sides of the bowl after each egg. Add the zucchini, and stir briefly to combine.

3) In a separate medium mixing bowl, combine the flour, baking soda, baking powder, cinnamon, nutmeg, and salt. Add flour mixture to butter-sugar mixture and mix briefly—just until ingredients have been incorporated.

4) Add the cranberries and walnuts and mix until just combined.

5) Transfer mixture to the prepared Bundt pan and spread batter evenly throughout the pan. Bake at 350 for 45–50 minutes, or until a toothpick comes out mostly clean.

6) Let the cake rest for 30 minutes, then turn out of the pan and allow to completely cool on a wire cooling rack.

—BANANA BREAD—

Bananas are tricky little guys—they act like a low-maintenance fruit, but before you've had a chance to eat half of the bunch they've turned brown and mushy. Luckily this recipe will take your huddled banana masses, yearning to be free, and give them a good home: your belly.

1/2 CUP BUTTER, ROOM TEMPERATURE

1 CUP SUGAR

2 EGGS, ROOM TEMPERATURE

1/2 TEASPOON VANILLA EXTRACT

3 VERY RIPE BANANAS, PEELED AND MASHED

1/2 CUP FLOUR

1 TEASPOON BAKING SODA

1/2 TEASPOON SALT

1) Preheat oven to 350 degrees. Liberally coat the Bundt pan with butter or canola oil spray and lightly flour, tapping out the excess flour to create a thin, even coat.

2) In a stand mixer with a paddle attachment, cream together the butter and sugar until the mixture is light and fluffy. Once finished, add the eggs one at a time and beat until thoroughly incorporated, scraping down the sides of the bowl after each egg. Add vanilla extract to your mixture, then add the bananas.

3) In a separate medium mixing bowl, combine the flour, baking soda and salt. Add flour mixture to butter-sugar mixture and mix briefly—just until ingredients have been incorporated.

4) Transfer mixture to the prepared Bundt pan and spread batter evenly throughout the pan. Bake at 350 for 45–50 minutes, or until a toothpick comes out mostly clean.

5) Let the cake rest for 30 minutes, then turn out of the pan and allow to completely cool on a wire cooling rack.

—BANANA NUT BREAD—

TIME: 70 MINUTES   SERVES: 8–10

Adding the crunch of nuts to banana bread goes a long way. The pecans in this recipe combined with the Vanilla Glaze (page 188) make this feel more like a decadent dessert than plain old banana bread!

1/2 CUP BUTTER, ROOM TEMPERATURE

1 CUP SUGAR

2 EGGS, ROOM TEMPERATURE

1/2 TEASPOON VANILLA EXTRACT

3 VERY RIPE BANANAS, PEELED AND MASHED

1/2 CUP FLOUR

1 TEASPOON BAKING SODA

1/2 TEASPOON SALT

1/2 CUP PECANS, CHOPPED, PLUS A FEW WHOLE PECANS FOR SERVING

VANILLA GLAZE (PAGE 188)

1) Preheat oven to 350 degrees. Liberally coat the Bundt pan with butter or canola oil spray and lightly flour, tapping out the excess flour to create a thin, even coat.

2) In a stand mixer with a paddle attachment, cream together the butter and sugar until the mixture is light and fluffy. Once finished, add the eggs one at a time and beat until thoroughly incorporated, scraping down the sides of the bowl after each egg. Add vanilla extract to your mixture, then add the bananas.

3) In a separate medium mixing bowl, combine the flour, baking soda and salt. Add flour mixture to butter-sugar mixture and mix briefly—just until ingredients have been incorporated.

4) Add the pecans and mix until just combined.

5) Transfer mixture to the prepared Bundt pan and spread batter evenly throughout the pan. Bake at 350 for 45–50 minutes, or until a toothpick comes out mostly clean.

6) Let the cake rest for 30 minutes, then turn out of the pan and allow to completely cool on a wire cooling rack. Top with whole pecans and Vanilla Glaze (page 188).

Looking to make this **BREAD INTO A DESSERT?**

TRY ADDING BUTTERSCOTCH OR TOFFEE CHIPS TO THE BATTER BEFORE PUTTING IT IN THE OVEN.

—CHOCOLATE BANANA BREAD—

TIME: 70 MINUTES   SERVES: 8–10

What's better than moist, sweet banana bread? Banana bread with chocolate, of course!

½ CUP BUTTER, ROOM TEMPERATURE

1 CUP SUGAR

2 EGGS, ROOM TEMPERATURE

½ TEASPOON VANILLA EXTRACT

3 VERY RIPE BANANAS, PEELED AND MASHED

2 TABLESPOONS COCOA POWDER

½ CUP FLOUR

1 TEASPOON BAKING SODA

½ TEASPOON SALT

1 CUP CHOCOLATE CHIPS

1) Preheat oven to 350 degrees. Liberally coat the Bundt pan with butter or canola oil spray and lightly flour, tapping out the excess flour to create a thin, even coat.

2) In a stand mixer with a paddle attachment, cream together the butter and sugar until the mixture is light and fluffy. Once finished, add the eggs one at a time and beat until thoroughly incorporated, scraping down the sides of the bowl after each egg. Add vanilla extract to your mixture, then add the bananas.

3) In a separate medium mixing bowl, combine the cocoa powder, flour, baking soda and salt.

4) Add the flour mixture to butter mixture, and pour in the chocolate chips. Mix briefly—just until ingredients have been incorporated.

5) Transfer mixture to the prepared Bundt pan and spread batter evenly throughout the pan. Bake at 350 for 45-50 minutes, or until a toothpick comes out mostly clean.

6) Let the cake rest for 30 minutes, then turn out of the pan and allow to completely cool on a wire cooling rack.

—GLUTEN-FREE BANANA OAT BREAD—

TIME: 70 MINUTES   SERVES: 8–10

Swapping oats and honey in this recipe is a natural alternative to make this recipe gluten-free.

½ CUP BUTTER, ROOM TEMPERATURE

1 CUP SUGAR

2 EGGS, ROOM TEMPERATURE

½ TEASPOON VANILLA EXTRACT

½ CUP HONEY

3 VERY RIPE BANANAS, PEELED AND MASHED

2 CUPS ROLLED OATS

1 TEASPOON BAKING SODA

½ TEASPOON SALT

1) Preheat oven to 350 degrees. Liberally coat the Bundt pan with butter or canola oil spray and lightly flour, tapping out the excess flour to create a thin, even coat.

2) In a stand mixer with a paddle attachment, cream together the butter and sugar until the mixture is light and fluffy. Once finished, add the eggs one at a time and beat until thoroughly incorporated, scraping down the sides of the bowl after each egg. Add vanilla extract to your mixture, then add the bananas and honey.

3) In a separate medium mixing bowl, combine the oats, baking soda, and salt. Add the oat mixture to butter-sugar mixture and mix until ingredients have been incorporated.

4) Transfer mixture to the prepared Bundt pan and spread batter evenly throughout the pan. Bake at 350 for 45–50 minutes, or until a toothpick comes out mostly clean.

5) Let the cake rest for 30 minutes, then turn out of the pan and allow to completely cool on a wire cooling rack.

—GINGERBREAD—

TIME: 70 MINUTES   SERVES: 8–10

The smell of this bread will absolutely put you in a holiday mood. The combination of spices and molasses is as wintery as it is tasty. Rather than decorating gingerbread cookies, try making a Bundt gingerbread, and decorate it to look like a wreath or cover it in sugary snowflakes. Everyone at your holiday party will be speechless!

1/2 CUP BUTTER, ROOM TEMPERATURE

1 CUP BROWN SUGAR

2 EGGS, ROOM TEMPERATURE

1/2 CUP MOLASSES

1 1/2 CUPS FLOUR

1 TEASPOON BAKING SODA

1/2 TEASPOON SALT

2 TEASPOONS GROUND GINGER

1 TEASPOON CINNAMON

1/4 TEASPOON GROUND CLOVES

1) Preheat oven to 350 degrees. Liberally coat the Bundt pan with butter or canola oil spray and lightly flour, tapping out the excess flour to create a thin, even coat.

2) In a stand mixer with a paddle attachment, cream together the butter and sugar until the mixture is fully combined. Once finished, add the eggs one at a time and beat until thoroughly incorporated, scraping down the sides of the bowl after each egg. Add the molasses and continue beating until well combined.

3) In a separate medium mixing bowl, combine the flour, baking soda, salt, ginger, cinnamon, and cloves. Add flour mixture to butter-sugar mixture and mix briefly—just until ingredients have been incorporated.

4) Transfer mixture to the prepared Bundt pan and spread batter evenly throughout the pan. Bake at 350 for 40-45 minutes, or until a toothpick comes out mostly clean.

5) Let the cake rest for 30 minutes, then turn out of the pan and allow to completely cool on a wire cooling rack.

Innovative Ideas:

HOLIDAY FLAIR

The Bundt's circular shape just begs to be decorated for every holiday. Pumpkins for autumn, baskets for spring, or snowballs for winter, the possibilities are only as limited as your decorating creativity! Bundts also make beautiful birthday cakes if you place the candles around the circle.

HERB GARDEN

This one goes hand in hand with all the cooking you're doing: Rather than buy rosemary, why not grow some right at home? The Bundt's unique circle shape will help your herb garden stand out against the boring terra cotta pots everybody else uses. Just be sure it gets as much natural light as possible.

Of course, you don't need to limit yourself to herbs. Succulents and most indoor plants will grow quite comfortably in a Bundt pan, provided their roots have room to grow. Not to mention that hooks and rope will transform the pan into a hanging pot that can go indoors or out! And if your plants outgrow the pan, well: You're going to need a bigger Bundt.

Desserts

Dessert doesn't just mean cake! Bundt pan desserts can be as innovative as any other kitchen utensil. The gorgeous design of the pan makes any dessert in it stand out, and is perfect for molding what may usually seem like boring desserts.

—CHERRY VANILLA JELL-O RING—

TIME: 2 HOURS PLUS 2 HOURS OF REFRIGERATION BEFORE SERVING
SERVES: 8–10

Jell-O doesn't have to be a boring dessert option! Jell-O is easy to mold into beautiful shapes, and adding fruit and pudding makes for a textured and exciting dessert.

2 CUPS WATER, DIVIDED

1 PACKAGE CHERRY GELATIN MIX

½ CUP MARASCHINO CHERRIES

1 PACKAGE VANILLA PUDDING MIX

2 CUPS COLD MILK

1) Boil 1 cup of water. Remove from heat, and combine the gelatin with the boiling water. Add the second cup of cold water and stir.

2) Pour the gelatin mix into the Bundt pan. Add the cherries throughout the gelatin. Refrigerate the gelatin for at least two hours.

3) Whisk the pudding mix and milk for at least five minutes, until pudding starts to set.

4) Layer the pudding over the gelatin layer and refrigerate for at least two hours before serving.

—BERRY WHITE CHOCOLATE JELL-O RING—

**TIME: 2 HOURS PLUS 2 HOURS OF REFRIGERATION BEFORE SERVING
SERVES: 8–10**

Jell-O doesn't have to be a boring dessert option! Jell-O is easy to mold into beautiful shapes, and adding fruit and pudding makes for a textured and exciting dessert.

2 CUPS WATER, DIVIDED

1 PACKAGE UNFLAVORED GELATIN

½ CUP BLUEBERRIES

½ CUP RASPBERRIES

1 PACKAGE WHITE CHOCOLATE PUDDING MIX

2 CUPS COLD MILK

1) Boil 1 cup of water. Remove from heat, and combine the gelatin with the boiling water. Add the second cup of cold water and stir.

2) Pour the gelatin mix into the Bundt pan. Add the blueberries and raspberries throughout the gelatin. Refrigerate the gelatin for at least two hours.

3) Whisk the pudding mix and milk for at least five minutes, until pudding starts to set.

4) Layer the pudding over the gelatin layer and refrigerate for at least two hours before serving.

FOR ADDED *Flare*

ADD IN EDIBLE FLOWERS TO THE GELATIN LAYER FOR A FLORAL TOUCH!

–STEWED CINNAMON APPLES–

TIME: 90 MINUTES   SERVES: 5

If you've got some Granny Smiths that are on the verge of going bad, don't fret. Slather them up with some cinnamon-sugar sweetness and pop them in the oven for a super easy, no-stress dessert.

5 GRANNY SMITH APPLES, CORED, ½ INCH SLICED OFF TOPS

1 ½ CUPS BUTTER, ROOM TEMPERATURE

¾ CUP BROWN SUGAR, DIVIDED

½ CUP GRANULATED SUGAR

1 TABLESPOON CINNAMON

½ TEASPOON SALT

1) Preheat oven to 350 degrees.

2) Core the apples all the way through using an apple corer. Cut ½ inch off the top of each apple.

3) In a mixing bowl, stir together butter, ½ cup brown sugar, granulated sugar, cinnamon and salt until evenly incorporated. Using a spoon, press the sugar mixture into the centers of each apple.

4) Place each apple in the Bundt pan and cover with foil. Bake for 60 minutes with the foil on.

5) Remove from heat and turn the oven up to 425 degrees. As the oven heats, take the foil off the Bundt pan and sprinkle ¼ cup brown sugar over the apples. When your oven is hot enough, place the pan back in the oven for 10–15 minutes, or until the sugar caramelizes.

6) Remove the pan from the oven and spoon the syrupy mixture from the bottom of the pan over the apples. Serve with cinnamon whipped cream or as is.

—BERRY CRUMBLE—

TIME: 60 MINUTES   SERVES: 10–12

This is the fruity goodness we all dream of in the winter months. Use fresh berries in the summer and frozen in the winter—either way, their warm juices will have you craving another slice. Serve warm or at room temperature with or without whipped cream.

½ CUP ALL-PURPOSE FLOUR

½ CUP LIGHT BROWN SUGAR

¼ CUP GRANULATED SUGAR

½ TEASPOON CINNAMON

¼ TEASPOON SALT

½ CUP OATS

6 TABLESPOONS COLD BUTTER, CHOPPED

4 CUPS MIXED BERRIES, FROZEN

½ CUP SUGAR

2 TABLESPOONS CORNSTARCH

1) Preheat the oven to 350 degrees. Liberally coat the Bundt pan with butter or canola oil spray.

2) In a large mixing bowl, combine flour, brown sugar, cinnamon, salt and oats.

3) Add the diced cold butter and, using patty blender, fork or your fingers, combine the butter with the dry ingredients until the mixture resembles rocky pebbles.

4) In a separate large mixing bowl, combine frozen berries, granulated sugar and cornstarch.

5) Pour berry mixture into the prepared Bundt pan, then top it with your crumble mixture.

6) Bake for 35-45 minutes, until the berries ooze juices and your crumble topping is a rich golden brown.

7) Serve warm with ice cream, or room temperature by itself.

—CARAMEL MOCHA ICE CREAM CAKE—

TIME: 60 MINUTES   SERVES: 8–10

Ice cream cake may seem like an easy dessert to make, but putting it in a Bundt pan ensures that it will be the perfect addition to any summer barbeque or birthday celebration.

1 PINT COFFEE ICE CREAM

1 PACKAGE CREAM-FILLED CHOCOLATE COOKIES

4 TABLESPOONS BUTTER, MELTED

1 BAR SEMI-SWEET CHOCOLATE

WHIPPED CREAM, FOR SERVING

CARAMEL SAUCE (PAGE 202), FOR SERVING

1) Line your Bundt pan with plastic wrap for easy cake removal.

2) Remove the ice cream from the refrigerator and allow it to soften for 10-15 minutes at room temperature.

3) Remove the cream filling from the chocolate cookies and place it in a bowl with the melted butter. Whisk together, heating slightly if necessary to help the cream become more pliable. Don't worry if the mixture doesn't become entirely smooth.

4) Place the chocolate cookies in a plastic bag and crush into fine crumbs. Pour the butter and cream mixture over the cookie crumbs.

5) Press about half of the crumbs in the bottom of the Bundt pan in a thin layer, reserving the other half. Press firmly and move up the sides of the Bundt pan slightly.

6) Scoop the softened ice cream on top of the crumb crust, pressing lightly with a spoon to flatten the top. Press the remaining cookie crumbs on top of the ice cream in a thin layer.

7) Place the Bundt pan in the freezer for 30–45 minutes so that the ice cream can re-harden. Use this time to make the Caramel Sauce (page 202).

8) When the ice cream cake has hardened, flip it over onto a plate to remove from the Bundt pan, and remove the plastic wrap.

9) Pour the Caramel Sauce over the cake, shave the bar of chocolate over the sauce, and top with whipped cream.

—NEAPOLITAN ICE CREAM CAKE—

TIME: 60 MINUTES   SERVES: 8–10

Neapolitan ice cream is a classic flavor combination that makes for a beautiful cake. Each layer is visible, and the Bundt pan's shape makes this a beautifully simple cake.

3 CUPS VANILLA ICE CREAM

3 CUPS CHOCOLATE ICE CREAM

3 CUPS STRAWBERRY ICE CREAM

2 CUPS GRAHAM CRACKER CRUMBS

4 TABLESPOONS BUTTER, MELTED

STRAWBERRY SAUCE, PAGE 205

1 BAR SEMI-SWEET CHOCOLATE

WHIPPED CREAM, FOR SERVING

1) Line your Bundt pan with plastic wrap for easy cake removal.

2) Remove the ice cream from the refrigerator and allow it to soften for 10-15 minutes at room temperature.

3) Scoop the vanilla ice cream into the bottom of the Bundt pan, pressing lightly with a spoon to smooth the top. Repeat with the chocolate ice cream. Repeat with the strawberry ice cream.

4) Pour the melted butter over the graham crackers and stir to combine. Press the mixture over the top of the ice cream in a thin, even layer.

5) Place the Bundt pan in the freezer for 30-45 minutes so that the ice cream can re-harden. Use this time to make the Strawberry Sauce (page 205).

6) When the ice cream cake has hardened, flip it over onto a plate to remove from the Bundt pan, and remove the plastic wrap.

7) Pour the Strawberry Sauce over the cake, shave the bar of chocolate over the sauce, and top with whipped cream.

—BANANA SPLIT ICE CREAM CAKE—

TIME: 60 MINUTES   SERVES: 8–10

A banana split is a classic and nostalgic dessert, and making it in a Bundt pan makes it incredibly easy to serve to a crowd.

½ CUP WALNUTS, CHOPPED

2 BANANAS, SLICED

¼ CUP CHOPPED MARASCHINO CHERRIES

3 CUPS VANILLA ICE CREAM

3 CUPS CHOCOLATE ICE CREAM

3 CUPS STRAWBERRY ICE CREAM

1 CUP CHOCOLATE SAUCE, FOR SERVING

WHIPPED CREAM, FOR SERVING

1) Line your Bundt pan with plastic wrap for easy cake removal.

2) Remove the ice cream from the refrigerator and allow it to soften for 10-15 minutes at room temperature.

3) Layer the walnuts, banana slices, and cherry pieces along the bottom of the Bundt pan. Feel free to get creative with how you place them for a more intricate design on the top of you Bundt when you flip it over.

4) Scoop the vanilla ice cream into the bottom of the Bundt pan, pressing lightly with a spoon to smooth the top. Repeat with the chocolate ice cream. Repeat with the strawberry ice cream.

5) Place the Bundt pan in the freezer for 30–45 minutes so that the ice cream can re-harden.

6) When the ice cream cake has hardened, flip it over onto a plate to remove from the Bundt pan, and remove the plastic wrap.

7) Pour the chocolate sauce over the cake and top with whipped cream.

FOR EVEN MORE *Flavor*

TRY TOPPING THIS TREAT WITH THE STRAWBERRY SAUCE FROM THE NEAPOLITAN ICE CREAM CAKE RECIPE (PAGE 106).

—ICE CREAM STUFFED CAKE—

TIME: 80 MINUTES   SERVES: 8–10

There a few combinations as classic as cake and ice cream, and this recipe combines them in a truly iconic way by putting them together.

1/2 CUP BUTTER, ROOM TEMPERATURE

1/2 CUP SUGAR

2 EGGS, ROOM TEMPERATURE

1 TEASPOON VANILLA EXTRACT

1 CUP GREEK YOGURT

2 1/2 CUPS ALL-PURPOSE FLOUR

1/2 TEASPOON BAKING SODA

1 TEASPOON BAKING POWDER

1/2 CUP COCOA POWDER

1/2 TEASPOON SALT

2 CUPS VANILLA BEAN ICE CREAM

CHOCOLATE GANACHE (PAGE 192)

1) Preheat the oven to 350 degrees. Liberally coat the Bundt pan with butter or canola oil spray and lightly flour, tapping out the excess flour to create a thin, even coat.

2) In a stand mixer with a paddle attachment, cream together the butter and sugar until light and fluffy. Once finished, add the eggs one at a time and beat until thoroughly incorporated, scraping down the sides of the bowls after each egg. Add vanilla extract and yogurt.

3) In a separate bowl, mix together all-purpose flour, baking soda, baking powder, cocoa powder, and salt. Add the flour mixture to butter/sugar/egg mixture, mixing just until incorporated.

4) Transfer cake batter to your prepared Bundt pan. Bake at 350 for 45-50 minutes, or until a toothpick comes out mostly clean.

5) Remove from heat. Let the cake to rest in the pan for up to 30 minutes, then turn out of the pan and allow to completely cool on a wire cooling rack.

6) Once the cake has cooled completely, cut it into two halves horizontally.

7) Using a spoon, scoop out a thin line in the middle of each layer to create a space for the ice cream. Be careful to leave the edges intact so that the ice cream doesn't leak out.

8) Spoon the ice cream into the hollow area you've just created. Replace the top layer of the cake and press down slightly to seal. Drizzle the cake with Chocolate Ganache (page 192) and eat immediately. Store any leftovers in the freezer.

—CHOCOLATE MINT STUFFED ICE CREAM CAKE—

TIME: 80 MINUTES   SERVES: 8–10

There's no need to choose between cake and ice cream with this decadent dessert! The iconic combination of chocolate and mint comes together perfectly in this loaded treat. Serving dessert to a crowd is simplified—there's no need to scoop ice cream for each person. Just cut the cake into thick slices for quick and easy serving!

½ CUP BUTTER, ROOM TEMPERATURE

½ CUP SUGAR

2 EGGS, ROOM TEMPERATURE

1 TEASPOON PEPPERMINT EXTRACT

1 CUP GREEK YOGURT

2 ½ CUPS ALL-PURPOSE FLOUR

½ TEASPOON BAKING SODA

1 TEASPOON BAKING POWDER

½ CUP COCOA POWDER

½ TEASPOON SALT

2 CUPS MINT CHOCOLATE CHIP ICE CREAM

CHOCOLATE GANACHE (PAGE 192)

1) Preheat the oven to 350 degrees. Liberally coat the Bundt pan with butter or canola oil spray and lightly flour, tapping out the excess flour to create a thin, even coat.

2) In a stand mixer with a paddle attachment, cream together the butter and sugar until light and fluffy. Once finished, add the eggs one at a time and beat until thoroughly incorporated, scraping down the sides of the bowls after each egg. Add peppermint extract and yogurt.

3) In a separate bowl, mix together all-purpose flour, baking soda, baking powder, cocoa powder, and salt. Add the flour mixture to butter/sugar/egg mixture, mixing just until incorporated.

4) Transfer cake batter to your prepared Bundt pan. Bake at 350 for 45-50 minutes, or until a toothpick comes out mostly clean.

5) Remove from heat. Let the cake to rest in the pan for up to 30 minutes, then turn out of the pan and allow to completely cool on a wire cooling rack.

6) Once the cake has cooled completely, cut it into two halves horizontally.

7) Using a spoon, scoop out a thin line in the middle of each layer to create a space for the ice cream. Be careful to leave the edges intact so that the ice cream doesn't leak out.

8) Spoon the ice cream into the hollow area you've just created. Replace the top layer of the cake and press down slightly to seal.

9) Drizzle the cake with Chocolate Ganache (page 192) and eat immediately. Store any leftovers in the freezer.

—RASPBERRY SORBET STUFFED POUND CAKE—

TIME: 80 MINUTES   SERVES: 8–10

This summery cake brings the buttery taste of pound cake and the tart taste of raspberry together perfectly. Serve this cake with a glass of lemonade for a guaranteed hit.

1 CUP BUTTER, ROOM TEMPERATURE

1 CUP SUGAR

5 EGGS, ROOM TEMPERATURE

1 TEASPOON VANILLA EXTRACT

JUICE FROM 1 LEMON

2 CUPS ALL-PURPOSE FLOUR

1 ½ TEASPOONS BAKING POWDER

½ TEASPOON SALT

2 CUPS RASPBERRY SORBET

1) Preheat the oven to 350 degrees. Liberally coat the Bundt pan with butter or canola oil spray and lightly flour, tapping out excess flour to create a thin, even coat.

2) In a stand mixer with a paddle attachment, cream together the butter and sugar until light and fluffy. Once finished, add the eggs one at a time and beat until thoroughly incorporated, scraping down the sides of the bowls after each egg. Add vanilla extract and lemon juice.

3) In a separate bowl, mix together all-purpose flour, baking powder and salt. Add this to egg mixture, mixing just until incorporated.

4) Transfer cake batter to the prepared Bundt pan. Bake at 350 for 45–50 minutes or until a toothpick comes out mostly clean.

5) Remove from heat and let the cake to rest in the pan for up to 30 minutes, then turn out of the pan and allow to completely cool on a wire cooling rack.

6) Once the cake has cooled completely, cut it into two halves horizontally.

7) Using a spoon, scoop out a thin line in the middle of each layer to create a space for the sorbet. Be careful to leave the edges intact so that the ice cream doesn't leak out.

8) Spoon the sorbet into the hollow area you've just created. Replace the top layer of the cake and press down slightly to seal.

—CREAM PUFF CAKE—

TIME: 60 MINUTES   SERVES: 8–10

This light and airy treat is a simple group version of traditional cream puff desserts. Using a Bundt not only makes a beautiful display, but also makes it easy to avoid unevenly-sized cream puffs. Even better, you won't need to fill each individual dessert by hand. Instead, the end result is a beautiful, layered ring.

½ CUP BUTTER

1 CUP WATER

1 CUP ALL-PURPOSE FLOUR

4 EGGS

2 CUPS WHIPPING CREAM

⅓ CUP CONFECTIONERS' SUGAR

¾ TEASPOON VANILLA EXTRACT

1) Preheat the oven to 375 degrees. Prepare your Bundt pan by liberally coating with butter or canola oil cooking spray.

2) Heat the butter and water in a large saucepan over medium-high heat until it begins to boil.

3) Once the mixture has boiled, reduce the heat to low and add the flour. Cook the mixture over low, stirring until the mixture forms a ball and pulls away from the pan. Remove from heat.

4) One at a time, add the eggs and beat the mixture well.

5) Transfer the mixture to the Bundt pan and bake for 40–45 minutes.

6) While the cake bakes, make the cream filling. Beat the cream in a large bowl using a beater or whisk until it starts to thicken. Add the sugar and vanilla, and continue beating until cream has reached a stiff consistency.

7) Allow the puff cake to cool completely, then flip the cake onto a plate.

8) Split the cake in half and add the cream to the bottom layer. Replace the top layer.

—MINI BUNDT PAN PANNA COTTA—

TIME: 15 MINUTES, PLUS FOUR HOURS REFRIGERATION BEFORE SERVING
SERVES: 6–8

Panna Cotta is a classic Italian dessert, and making it in a Bundt makes it into perfect individual serving sizes.

2 ENVELOPES UNFLAVORED GELATIN

1 CUP MILK

2 CUPS HEAVY CREAM

1 CUP GRANULATED SUGAR

1 TEASPOON VANILLA EXTRACT

1) In a small bowl, combine the milk and gelatin. Set aside.

2) In a saucepan over medium heat, stir together the heavy cream and sugar, watching carefully. When the mixture comes to a full boil, add the gelatin mixture and stir until completely dissolved, and then cook for one minute stirring continuously.

3) Remove from the heat and add the vanilla. Stir to combine, and pour into the mini Bundt pan. Allow to cool at room temperature.

4) Cover the pan with plastic wrap when cool and refrigerate for at least 4 hours before serving.

—MINI BUNDT PAN STRAWBERRY PANNA COTTA—

TIME: 15 MINUTES, PLUS FOUR HOURS REFRIGERATION BEFORE SERVING   SERVES: 6–8

Panna Cotta and strawberries are a perfect fit. Individual serving sizes make this treat a hit at parties and dinner parties.

2 ENVELOPES UNFLAVORED GELATIN

1 CUP MILK

2 CUPS HEAVY CREAM

1 CUP GRANULATED SUGAR

1 TEASPOON VANILLA EXTRACT

½ CUP STRAWBERRIES, CRUSHED

FOR THE STRAWBERRY SAUCE:

2 CUPS STRAWBERRIES, SLICED

½ CUP SUGAR

1 TEASPOON VANILLA EXTRACT

1) In a small bowl, combine the milk and gelatin. Set aside.

2) In a saucepan over medium heat, stir together the heavy cream and sugar, watching carefully. When the mixture comes to a full boil, add the gelatin mixture and stir until completely dissolved, and then cook for one minute stirring continuously.

3) Remove from the heat and add the vanilla and strawberries. Stir to combine, and pour into the mini Bundt pan. Allow to cool at room temperature.

4) Cover the pan with plastic wrap when cool and refrigerate for at least 4 hours before serving.

5) For the Strawberry Sauce, mix the strawberries, sugar, and vanilla together in a saucepan. Cook over medium-low heat for about 10–15 minutes until the sauce thickens, stirring occasionally and mashing the strawberries lightly with a wooden spoon. For a sauce with fewer strawberry chunks, puree in a blender to desired consistency.

—FLAN—

TIME: 90 MINUTES   SERVES: 8–10

Flan is a classic dessert recipe that is made incredibly beautiful with the decorative edging of the Bundt pan. Flipping this cake out of the pan is half the fun, so present it in the pan to your guest and flip it at the table once you feel confident about it! In order for this cake to cook properly it needs to be made in a water bath, so make sure to have a large roasting pan on hand.

1/3 CUP CARAMEL SAUCE
(PAGE 202)

3/4 CUP BUTTER, ROOM
TEMPERATURE

1 1/3 CUPS SUGAR

2 EGGS, ROOM
TEMPERATURE

1 CUP BUTTERMILK

1 TEASPOON VANILLA
EXTRACT

1 3/4 CUPS ALL-PURPOSE
FLOUR

2/3 CUP DUTCH-PROCESSED
COCOA POWDER

1/2 TEASPOON SALT

2 TEASPOONS BAKING SODA

1 CAN (14 OUNCES)
SWEETENED CONDENSED
MILK

1 CUP MILK

4 EGGS

1 TEASPOON VANILLA
EXTRACT

1) Preheat the oven to 350 degrees. Prepare the Bundt pan by liberally coating with cooking spray to prevent sticking.

2) Pour the Caramel Sauce (page 202) into the bottom of the Bundt pan.

3) In a stand mixer with a paddle attachment, cream together the butter and sugar until the mixture is light and fluffy. Once finished, add the eggs one at a time and beat until thoroughly incorporated, scraping down the sides of the bowl after each egg. Add vanilla extract.

4) In a separate medium mixing bowl, combine flour, cocoa powder, baking soda, and salt.

5) Add 1/3 of the flour mixture to the stand mixer bowl with the butter-sugar mixture. Then add 1/3 of the buttermilk to the stand mixer bowl. Repeat this process, alternating between adding dry ingredients and buttermilk.

6) Transfer the cake batter mixture to the prepared Bundt pan over the Caramel Sauce.

7) Beat the condensed milk, milk, eggs, and vanilla in a blender or with a beater until thoroughly combined. Pour the mixture over the batter in the pan. The cake and flan layers will initially combine, but will separate during cooking.

8) Place the Bundt pan in a roasting pan with about 1 inch of water. Tent the Bundt with aluminum foil. Place the roasting pan with the water and Bundt in the oven.

9) Bake at 350 for 60-70 minutes, or until a toothpick comes out of the cake layer mostly clean.

10) Allow to cool for 5-10 minutes before turning over onto a plate.

-CHEESECAKE-

TIME: 95 MINUTES +2 HOURS OF REFRIGERATION BEFORE SERVING
SERVES: 8–10

Yeah, you read that right: Bundt cheesecake! You know how the edges of a cheesecake are a little thick and chewy? Imagine twice the crust, and twice the edge, and you get this decadent treat.

2 TABLESPOONS GRANULATED SUGAR

1/3 CUP BUTTER, MELTED

1 1/3 CUPS GRAHAM CRACKER CRUMBLES

5 1/2 8-OUNCE PACKAGES CREAM CHEESE

1/4 TEASPOON SALT

3/4 CUP SUGAR

6 EGGS, ROOM TEMPERATURE

1/3 CUP WHIPPING CREAM

1) Preheat the oven to 300 degrees. Liberally coat the Bundt pan with butter or canola oil spray and lightly flour, tapping out the excess flour to create a thin, even coat.

2) In a bowl, mix together the sugar, butter and graham cracker crumbs. Press this mixture into the bottom of your prepared Bundt pan—no more than ½ inch up the sides of the pan. Bake for 10 minutes, then set aside.

3) In a stand mixer with a paddle attachment, mix together the cream cheese, sugar, and salt. Once finished, add the eggs one at a time, scraping down the sides of the bowl after each egg. Add the whipping cream to the mix and scrape down the sides one last time.

4) Transfer cheesecake batter to the prepared Bundt pan. Bake for 75 minutes.

5) Remove and let cool for 20 minutes before transferring the pan to the fridge. Allow to rest in the fridge for 2 hours, or ideally overnight.

6) Serve chilled or at room temperature by itself or with Raspberry Lemon Sauce (page 206).

—CHOCOLATE CHERRY CHEESECAKE—

TIME: 95 MINUTES +2 HOURS OF REFRIGERATION BEFORE SERVING
SERVES: 8–10

The only thing that could possibly make Bundt cheesecake better is an abundance of chocolate! This chocolate and cherry combination is decadently sinful.

2 TABLESPOONS GRANULATED SUGAR

1/3 CUP BUTTER, MELTED

1 1/3 CUPS CHOCOLATE COOKIE CRUMBLES

5 1/2 8-OUNCE PACKAGES CREAM CHEESE

3/4 CUP SUGAR

2 TABLESPOONS COCOA POWDER

1/4 TEASPOON SALT

6 EGGS, ROOM TEMPERATURE

1/3 CUP WHIPPING CREAM

1/2 CUP CHOCOLATE CHIPS

1/2 CUP CHOPPED CHERRIES

1) Preheat the oven to 300 degrees. Liberally coat the Bundt pan with butter or canola oil spray and lightly flour, tapping out the excess flour to create a thin, even coat.

2) In a bowl, mix together the sugar, butter and chocolate cookie crumbs. Press this mixture into the bottom of your prepared Bundt pan—no more than ½ inch up the sides of the pan. Bake for 10 minutes, then set aside.

3) In a stand mixer with a paddle attachment, mix together the cream cheese, sugar, cocoa powder, and salt. Once finished, add the eggs one at a time, scraping down the sides of the bowl after each egg. Add the whipping cream, chocolate chips, and cherry pieces to the mix, combine, and scrape down the sides one last time.

4) Transfer cheesecake batter to the prepared Bundt pan. Bake for 75 minutes.

5) Remove and let cool for 20 minutes before transferring the pan to the fridge. Allow to rest in the fridge for 2 hours, or ideally overnight.

—CHEESECAKE FILLED CHOCOLATE CAKE—

TIME: 70 MINUTES   SERVES: 8–10

What could be better than combining two classic desserts: cheesecake and chocolate cake?
This crowd pleaser is easy to adapt for your favorite fillings and cake recipes too.

½ CUP BUTTER, ROOM TEMPERATURE

½ CUP SUGAR

2 EGGS, ROOM TEMPERATURE

1 TEASPOON VANILLA EXTRACT

1 CUP GREEK YOGURT

2 ½ CUPS ALL-PURPOSE FLOUR

½ TEASPOON BAKING SODA

1 TEASPOON BAKING POWDER

½ CUP COCOA POWDER

½ TEASPOON SALT

1 PACKAGE (8 OUNCES) CREAM CHEESE

¾ CUP CONDENSED MILK

1 TEASPOON VANILLA EXTRACT

½ CUP FRESH STRAWBERRIES, DICED

1) Preheat the oven to 350 degrees. Liberally coat the Bundt pan with butter or canola oil spray and lightly flour, tapping out the excess flour to create a thin, even coat.

2) In a stand mixer with a paddle attachment, cream together the butter and sugar until light and fluffy. Once finished, add the eggs one at a time and beat until thoroughly incorporated, scraping down the sides of the bowls after each egg. Add vanilla extract and yogurt.

3) In a separate bowl, mix together all-purpose flour, baking soda, baking powder, cocoa powder, and salt. Add the flour mixture to butter/sugar/egg mixture, mixing just until incorporated.

4) Transfer cake batter to your prepared Bundt pan. Bake at 350 for 45–50 minutes, or until a toothpick comes out mostly clean.

5) Let the cake to rest in the pan for up to 30 minutes, then turn out of the pan and allow to completely cool on a wire cooling rack.

6) While the cake is baking, make the cheesecake filling. Beat the cream cheese with a beater and slowly add the condensed milk. Continue beating until combined. Add the vanilla and strawberries and beat until just combined.

7) Once the cake has cooled completely, cut it into two halves horizontally.

8) Using a spoon, scoop out a thin line in the middle of each layer to create a space for the cheesecake. Be careful to leave the edges intact so that the cheesecake doesn't leak out. Spoon the cheesecake into the hollow area you've just created. Replace the top layer of the cake and press down slightly to seal.

Innovative Ideas:

PARTY DIP

For pull-apart breads and party appetizers, the Bundt's center makes the perfect vessel for a dipping sauce. Just pour a sauce, glaze, or frosting into a small bowl, and place it in the middle. This makes serving a crowd so easy! Try it with Sticky Buns (page 18) or Cheddar Ranch Pull-Apart Bread (page 71).

ROASTING PAN

Bundt pans are absolutely not dessert-specific. In fact, much like any other pan, they can be used for roasting in the oven. Your vegetables have never looked better. But, there's also a sneaky trick that makes the Bundt pan a great chicken-roasting tool. Place the chicken's center cavity over the hole in the middle of the Bundt pan so that it stands up straight. Then, fill the Bundt with your favorite fragrant vegetables. The chicken will flavor the vegetables and vice versa for one heavenly roast. Just make sure you place aluminum foil or a drip pan under the Bundt to keep your oven clean.

GIFT WRAP CARRIER

Store or carry all your gift wrapping supplies in one place! Stuff the pan with bows and tape, and wrap ribbons around the center hole. The center is also a great place for scissors!

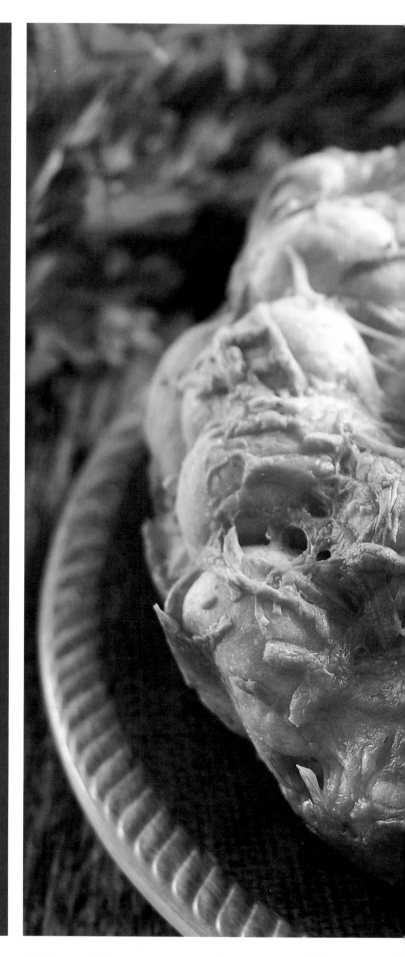

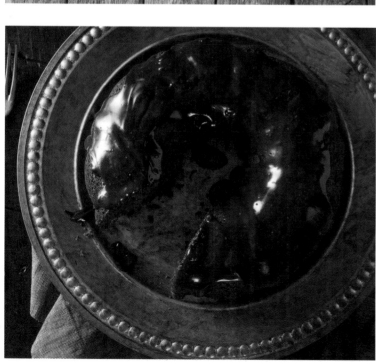

Cakes

No Bundt-made meal would be complete without a delicious and interesting final course. Still, cake-baking is a tightrope walk that can frustrate even the most accomplished cook. The good news? If you're using whole, lovely ingredients to start with, you will get tasty, mind-blowing treats with a fraction of the work.

Cake Commandments:

1) USE ROOM TEMPERATURE BUTTER. It's simple: Room temperature butter creams together with sugar more easily than cold butter, incorporating more air and leading to a more tender cake.

2) USE ROOM TEMPERATURE EGGS. This goes hand in hand with step one; in the creaming method's order of operations, we cream together the butter and sugar, and then we add the eggs. If cold eggs get added to room temperature butter, the butter will cool down—halting the air incorporation that would have happened otherwise.

3) USE A STAND MIXER WITH A PADDLE ATTACHMENT. We totally understand that some people do not have a stand mixer (the classic KitchenAid model with a stainless steel bowl is our go-to), and that won't stop you from making some awesome cakes. Simply use a handheld mixer or be ready to put some serious bicep strength into the process of whisking the butter and sugar together. There's nothing wrong with getting a workout in while you bake! That being said, if you have the funds and you've been on the fence, we highly recommend a standing mixer. It's so versatile, and you'll probably end up using it more than you think.

4) AVOID THE DREADED OVER-MIXED BATTER. Over-mixing is such a common mistake—even among professional bakers—and it's not a clearly measurable benchmark. It takes time to develop a sense of when your batter is properly mixed. The simplest rule of thumb: You can always mix it a little more, but you cannot unmix it. The dicey moment comes as you add flour to your egg mixture. Wheat-based flours rely on gluten, their protein strand, to mix with the liquids and fats and give the cake its strength. And that's great—until the gluten strands are over-incorporated and the cake becomes tough instead of tender. If you're nervous about over-mixing, use a rubber spatula to incorporate the flour/dry ingredients just until combined (meaning just until you don't see any dry bits remaining). This commandment is key to making a moist, tender cake instead of a dried-out hockey puck.

5) ONLY USE UNSALTED BUTTER IN DESSERTS. All of these recipes call for unsalted butter because we like to be in control of how much salt we add to our recipes. Every brand of salted butter uses a different amount of salt. Because we are unable to be in your kitchen or the grocery store with you every step of the way, we opted to use unsalted butter and then add an easily measurable amount of kosher salt to the recipe when appropriate.

—VANILLA CAKE—

TIME: 60 MINUTES   SERVES: 8–10

Vanilla cake is a classic for a reason. Baking a basic cake in a Bundt pan is a surefire way to ensure the most beautiful cake your guests have ever seen. Pair this recipe with any of the options in the Glazes, Sauces, and Frostings (page 186) section for a guaranteed success!

3/4 CUP BUTTER, ROOM TEMPERATURE

1 1/3 CUPS SUGAR

2 EGGS, ROOM TEMPERATURE

1 CUP BUTTERMILK

1 TEASPOON VANILLA EXTRACT

1 3/4 CUPS ALL-PURPOSE FLOUR

1/2 TEASPOON SALT

2 TEASPOONS BAKING SODA

1) Preheat oven to 350 degrees. Liberally coat the Bundt pan with butter or canola oil spray and lightly flour, tapping out the excess flour to create a thin, even coat.

2) In a stand mixer with a paddle attachment, cream together the butter and sugar until the mixture is light and fluffy. Once finished, add the eggs one at a time and beat until thoroughly incorporated, scraping down the sides of the bowl after each egg. Add vanilla extract.

3) In a separate medium mixing bowl, combine flour, baking soda, and salt.

4) Add 1/3 of the flour mixture to the stand mixer bowl with the butter-sugar mixture. Then add 1/3 of the buttermilk to the stand mixer bowl. Repeat this process, alternating between adding dry ingredients and buttermilk.

5) Transfer the cake batter mixture to the prepared Bundt pan and spread batter evenly throughout the pan.

6) Bake at 350 for 45-50 minutes, or until a toothpick comes out mostly clean.

7) Allow the cake to rest in the pan for up to 30 minutes, then turn out of the pan and allow to completely cool on a wire cooling rack.

8) Once cooled, dust with powdered sugar using a fine meshed sieve.

—GLUTEN-FREE VANILLA CAKE—

TIME: 60 MINUTES   SERVES: 8–10

Everyone should be able to enjoy vanilla cake! This basic cake can be used as a base for many of the other creative combinations.

3/4 CUP BUTTER, ROOM TEMPERATURE

1 1/3 CUPS SUGAR

2 EGGS, ROOM TEMPERATURE

1 CUP BUTTERMILK

1 TEASPOON VANILLA EXTRACT

2 CUPS GLUTEN-FREE FLOUR

1 TEASPOON XANTHAN GUM

1/2 TEASPOON SALT

2 TEASPOONS BAKING SODA

1) Preheat oven to 350 degrees. Liberally coat the Bundt pan with butter or canola oil spray and lightly flour, tapping out the excess flour to create a thin, even coat.

2) In a stand mixer with a paddle attachment, cream together the butter and sugar until the mixture is light and fluffy. Once finished, add the eggs one at a time and beat until thoroughly incorporated, scraping down the sides of the bowl after each egg. Add vanilla extract.

3) In a separate medium mixing bowl, combine flour, baking soda, and salt.

4) Add ⅓ of the flour mixture to the stand mixer bowl with the butter-sugar mixture. Then add ⅓ of the buttermilk to the stand mixer bowl. Repeat this process, alternating between adding dry ingredients and buttermilk.

5) Transfer the cake batter mixture to the prepared Bundt pan and spread batter evenly throughout the pan.

6) Bake at 350 for 45–50 minutes, or until a toothpick comes out mostly clean.

7) Allow the cake to rest in the pan for up to 30 minutes, then turn out of the pan and allow to completely cool on a wire cooling rack.

8) Once cooled, dust with powdered sugar using a fine meshed sieve.

—BUTTERMILK POUND CAKE—

TIME: 70 MINUTES   SERVES: 8–10

Far too simple to taste this delicious, this cake is perfect for the unexpecting host. Old friend in town? Mother-in-law wants to drop by in an hour? Thin out a raspberry jam (or strawberry, or whatever you have on hand) with a little lemon juice and maybe a touch of salt, then slather up a slice of tangy, moist pound cake to impress the socks off of whoever just "happened to be in the neighborhood."

¾ CUP BUTTER, ROOM TEMPERATURE

1 CUP SUGAR

3 EGGS, ROOM TEMPERATURE

1 TEASPOON VANILLA EXTRACT

1 CUP + 2 TABLESPOONS BUTTERMILK

2 CUPS ALL-PURPOSE FLOUR

1 ½ TEASPOONS BAKING POWDER

½ TEASPOON SALT

RASPBERRY LEMON SAUCE (PAGE 206)

1) Preheat oven to 350 degrees. Liberally coat the Bundt pan with butter or canola oil spray and lightly flour, tapping out the excess flour to ensure a thin, even coat.

2) In a stand mixer with a paddle attachment, cream together the butter and sugar until the mixture is light and fluffy. Once finished, add the eggs one at a time and beat until thoroughly incorporated, scraping down the sides of the bowl after each addition. Add the vanilla extract.

3) In a separate medium mixing bowl, combine flour, baking powder and salt.

4) Add ⅓ of the flour mixture to the butter-sugar mixture. Then add ⅓ of the buttermilk to the stand mixer bowl. Repeat the process, alternating between adding the dry ingredients and buttermilk.

5) Transfer mixture to the prepared Bundt pan and spread batter evenly throughout the pan.

6) Bake at 350 for 45-50 minutes or until a toothpick comes out mostly clean.

7) Allow the cake to rest in the pan for up to 30 minutes, then turn out of the pan and allow to fully cool on a wire cooling rack. Top with Raspberry Lemon Sauce (page 206) before serving.

—LEMON POUND CAKE—

TIME: 70 MINUTES   SERVES: 8–10

Lemon is the perfect light flavor to match the density of pound cake. Try this delicious cake with a simple Vanilla Glaze (page 188), or use a glaze with whatever flavors you like best with lemon.

¾ CUP BUTTER, ROOM TEMPERATURE

1 CUP SUGAR

3 EGGS, ROOM TEMPERATURE

1 TEASPOON VANILLA EXTRACT

¼ CUP LEMON JUICE

1 CUP BUTTERMILK

2 CUPS ALL-PURPOSE FLOUR

1 ½ TEASPOONS BAKING POWDER

½ TEASPOON SALT

ZEST FROM 1 LEMON

1) Preheat oven to 350 degrees. Liberally coat the Bundt pan with butter or canola oil spray and lightly flour, tapping out the excess flour to ensure a thin, even coat.

2) In a stand mixer with a paddle attachment, cream together the butter and sugar until the mixture is light and fluffy. Once finished, add the eggs one at a time and beat until thoroughly incorporated, scraping down the sides of the bowl after each addition. Add the vanilla extract and lemon juice.

3) In a separate medium mixing bowl, combine flour, baking powder and salt.

4) Add ⅓ of the flour mixture to the butter-sugar mixture. Then add ⅓ of the buttermilk to the stand mixer bowl. Repeat the process, alternating between adding the dry ingredients and buttermilk.

5) Add the lemon zest and mix until just combined.

6) Transfer mixture to the prepared Bundt pan and spread batter evenly throughout the pan.

7) Bake at 350 for 45–50 minutes or until a toothpick comes out mostly clean.

8) Allow the cake to rest in the pan for up to 30 minutes, then turn out of the pan and allow to fully cool on a wire cooling rack.

—ROSEWATER POUND CAKE—

TIME: 70 MINUTES   SERVES: 8–10

Heads up! This cake will score you loads of fancy points with your friends. You're sure to be the star of the dinner party with this exotic-seeming dessert. Rosewater brings a floral component without tasting soapy, and fresh vanilla beans, while perhaps indulgent, are well worth the extra few bucks.

1 CUP BUTTER, ROOM TEMPERATURE

1 CUP SUGAR

5 EGGS, ROOM TEMPERATURE

2 TEASPOONS ROSE WATER

2 CUPS ALL-PURPOSE FLOUR

1 1/2 TEASPOONS BAKING POWDER

1/2 TEASPOON SALT

VANILLA PEACH COMPOTE (PAGE 206)

1) Preheat oven to 350 degrees. Liberally coat the Bundt pan with butter or canola oil spray and lightly flour, tapping out the excess flour to create a thin, even coat.

2) In a stand mixer with a paddle attachment, cream together the butter and sugar until the mixture is light and fluffy. Once finished, add the eggs one at a time and beat until thoroughly incorporated, scraping down the sides of the bowl after each egg. Add the 5 teaspoons of rosewater.

3) In a separate medium mixing bowl, combine flour, baking powder and salt.

4) Add the flour mixture to the egg mixture and mix briefly—just enough to incorporate all ingredients.

5) Transfer the combined mixture to your prepared Bundt pan and spread batter evenly throughout the pan. Bake at 350 for 45-50 minutes, or until a toothpick comes out mostly clean.

6) Allow the cake to rest in the pan for up to 30 minutes, then turn out of the pan and allow to completely cool on a wire cooling rack.

7) Serve with your Vanilla Peach Compote (page 206) on individual slices.

—STRAWBERRY BUNDT LAYER CAKE—

TIME: 80 MINUTES   SERVES: 8–10

The best thing about Bundt cakes is their ability to wow a crowd like a labored-over layer cake without any of the hard work. With just one cut, this fabulous cake combines both worlds to offer that double-wow factor. Strawberry shortcake is allowed to get messy, so don't worry if the whipped cream seems to be oozing too much—a little ooze just adds to the eater's amazement.

1 CUP BUTTER, ROOM
TEMPERATURE

1 CUP SUGAR

5 EGGS, ROOM
TEMPERATURE

1 TEASPOON VANILLA
EXTRACT

2 CUPS ALL-PURPOSE
FLOUR

1 1/2 TEASPOONS BAKING
POWDER

1/2 TEASPOON SALT

FOR FILLING:

1 PINT STRAWBERRIES,
SLICED

1 PINT WHIPPING CREAM

1 CUP POWDERED SUGAR

1/4 TEASPOON SALT

1/2 TEASPOON VANILLA
EXTRACT

THIS RECIPE IS A BIT
TIME SENSITIVE. IF IT
SITS TOO LONG AT ROOM
TEMPERATURE, THE
WHIPPED CREAM WILL
GET MELTY AND SAD. THE
CAKE CAN BE MADE UP TO
A DAY IN ADVANCE IF YOU
DECORATE WITH WHIPPED
CREAM AND STRAWBERRIES
JUST BEFORE SERVING.

1) Preheat the oven to 350 degrees. Liberally coat the Bundt pan with butter or canola oil spray and lightly flour, tapping out excess flour to create a thin, even coat.

2) Rinse strawberries thoroughly and slice. Set aside any especially pretty slices to use for the top, decorative layer.

3) In a stand mixer with a paddle attachment, cream together the butter and sugar until light and fluffy. Once finished, add the eggs one at a time and beat until thoroughly incorporated, scraping down the sides of the bowls after each egg. Add vanilla extract.

4) In a separate bowl, mix together all-purpose flour, baking powder and salt. Add this to egg mixture, mixing just until incorporated.

5) Transfer cake batter to the prepared Bundt pan. Bake at 350 for 45-50 minutes or until a toothpick comes out mostly clean.

6) Remove from heat and let the cake to rest in the pan for up to 30 minutes, then turn out of the pan and allow to completely cool on a wire cooling rack.

7) While the pound cake bakes, add the cold whipping cream to a stand mixer with a whisk attachment and turn on low speed. Then slowly add the powdered sugar to the whipping cream and turn on medium speed. Finally, add the salt and vanilla extract to the whipping cream and turn on highest speed until the whipped cream holds medium peaks (when the whisk leaves the whipped cream, the whipped cream should hold shape but gently fall over to one side). Careful not to whip too long or else it will curdle.

8) When the pound cake is completely cool, use a serrated knife to mark the vertical midpoint of the cake all the way around, turning the plate slowly with one hand in order to mark the cake all the way around. This line will serve as your guideline as you cut the cake in half. Cut along the midpoint using a sawing motion.

9) Set the top half of the cake aside. Spoon whipped cream onto the bottom half of the cake and spread evenly. Tightly place sliced strawberries in a single layer on top of the whipped cream, then add another thin layer of whipped cream on top of the strawberries.

10) Turn the top half of the cake upside down and place on top of the whipped cream and strawberry layer. Spoon whipped cream onto the top of top layer of cake and place your prettiest strawberries on top. Dust with powdered sugar and serve.

-PIÑA COLADA CAKE-

TIME: 60 MINUTES   SERVES: 8–10

This drink-inspired recipe will have you imagining you're sitting on a beach under a palm tree!

3/4 CUP BUTTER, ROOM TEMPERATURE

1 1/3 CUPS SUGAR

2 EGGS, ROOM TEMPERATURE

1 CUP BUTTERMILK

1 TEASPOON VANILLA EXTRACT

1 3/4 CUPS ALL-PURPOSE FLOUR

1/2 TEASPOON SALT

2 TEASPOONS BAKING SODA

1/2 CUP SHREDDED COCONUT

1/2 CUP CRUSHED PINEAPPLE

1) Preheat oven to 350 degrees. Liberally coat the Bundt pan with butter or canola oil spray and lightly flour, tapping out the excess flour to create a thin, even coat.

2) In a stand mixer with a paddle attachment, cream together the butter and sugar until the mixture is light and fluffy. Once finished, add the eggs one at a time and beat until thoroughly incorporated, scraping down the sides of the bowl after each egg. Add vanilla extract.

3) In a separate medium mixing bowl, combine flour, baking soda, and salt.

4) Add 1/3 of the flour mixture to the stand mixer bowl with the butter-sugar mixture. Then add 1/3 of the buttermilk to the stand mixer bowl. Repeat this process, alternating between adding dry ingredients and buttermilk.

5) Add the coconut and pineapple and stir until just combined.

6) Transfer the cake batter mixture to the prepared Bundt pan and spread batter evenly throughout the pan.

7) Bake at 350 for 45–50 minutes, or until a toothpick comes out mostly clean.

8) Allow the cake to rest in the pan for up to 30 minutes, then turn out of the pan and allow to completely cool on a wire cooling rack.

9) Once cooled, dust with powdered sugar using a fine meshed sieve.

—TRIPLE BERRY CAKE—

TIME: 60 MINUTES   SERVES: 8–10

This fruity combination is light, airy, and delicious. Eating it feels like a summer picnic.

¾ CUP BUTTER, ROOM TEMPERATURE

1 ⅓ CUPS SUGAR

2 EGGS, ROOM TEMPERATURE

1 CUP BUTTERMILK

1 TEASPOON VANILLA EXTRACT

1 ¾ CUPS ALL-PURPOSE FLOUR

½ TEASPOON SALT

2 TEASPOONS BAKING SODA

½ CUP BLUEBERRIES

½ CUP RASPBERRIES

½ CUP BLACKBERRIES

1) Preheat oven to 350 degrees. Liberally coat the Bundt pan with butter or canola oil spray and lightly flour, tapping out the excess flour to create a thin, even coat.

2) In a stand mixer with a paddle attachment, cream together the butter and sugar until the mixture is light and fluffy. Once finished, add the eggs one at a time and beat until thoroughly incorporated, scraping down the sides of the bowl after each egg. Add vanilla extract.

3) In a separate medium mixing bowl, combine flour, baking soda, and salt.

4) Add ⅓ of the flour mixture to the stand mixer bowl with the butter-sugar mixture. Then add ⅓ of the buttermilk to the stand mixer bowl. Repeat this process, alternating between adding dry ingredients and buttermilk.

5) Add the blueberries, raspberries, and blackberries. Mix until just combined.

6) Transfer the cake batter mixture to the prepared Bundt pan and spread batter evenly throughout the pan.

7) Bake at 350 for 45-50 minutes, or until a toothpick comes out mostly clean.

8) Allow the cake to rest in the pan for up to 30 minutes, then turn out of the pan and allow to completely cool on a wire cooling rack.

9) Once cooled, dust with powdered sugar using a fine meshed sieve.

—ORANGE CRANBERRY CAKE—

TIME: 80 MINUTES   SERVES: 8–10

Cranberries and oranges go together any time of year. Add more baking spices during the fall months for a cozier cake (think nutmeg and allspice) or keep it light and fresh with just a drizzle of this Orange Zest Glaze (page 196)

1 CUP CRANBERRIES, DRIED OR FROZEN

1 TABLESPOON ORANGE JUICE

1/2 CUP BUTTER, ROOM TEMPERATURE

1/2 CUP SUGAR

2 EGGS, ROOM TEMPERATURE

1 TEASPOON VANILLA EXTRACT

1/4 CUP GREEK YOGURT

1 TABLESPOON ORANGE ZEST

2 1/2 CUPS ALL-PURPOSE FLOUR

1 TEASPOON BAKING POWDER

1/2 TEASPOON BAKING SODA

1/2 TEASPOON SALT

1/2 TEASPOON GROUND CINNAMON

ORANGE ZEST GLAZE (PAGE 196)

1) Preheat oven to 350 degrees. Liberally coat the Bundt pan with butter or canola oil spray and lightly flour, tapping out the excess flour to create a thin, even coat.

2) In a small saucepan, bring the cranberries and 1 tablespoon of orange juice to a boil, then transfer to a small mixing bowl and let cool.

3) In a stand mixer with a paddle attachment, cream together the butter and sugar until the mixture is light and fluffy. Once finished, add eggs one at a time and beat until thoroughly incorporated, scraping down the sides of the bowl after each egg. Add the vanilla extract, followed by the Greek yogurt.

4) In a separate medium mixing bowl, combine flour, baking powder, baking soda, salt and cinnamon. Add the flour mixture to the butter/sugar/egg mixture, mixing briefly, just enough to incorporate all ingredients.

5) Add the cooled cranberry mixture to the batter, using a rubber spatula to incorporate. This will help avoid over-mixing!

6) Transfer mixture to the prepared Bundt pan and spread batter evenly throughout the pan. Bake at 350 for 50-55 minutes or until a toothpick comes out mostly clean.

7) Allow the cake to rest in the pan for up to 30 minutes, then turn out of the pan and allow to completely cool on a wire cooling rack.

—CINNAMON CRANBERRY CAKE—

TIME: 80 MINUTES   SERVES: 8–10

This delicious combination is a perfect holiday treat. The cinnamon and cranberries are a sweet pairing that smell heavenly in the oven.

1 CUP CRANBERRIES, DRIED OR FROZEN

1/2 CUP BUTTER, ROOM TEMPERATURE

1/2 CUP SUGAR

2 EGGS, ROOM TEMPERATURE

1 TEASPOON VANILLA EXTRACT

1/4 CUP GREEK YOGURT

2 1/2 CUPS ALL-PURPOSE FLOUR

1 TEASPOON BAKING POWDER

1/2 TEASPOON BAKING SODA

1/2 TEASPOON SALT

1 1/2 TEASPOONS GROUND CINNAMON

CINNAMON GLAZE (PAGE 201)

1) Preheat oven to 350 degrees. Liberally coat the Bundt pan with butter or canola oil spray and lightly flour, tapping out the excess flour to create a thin, even coat.

2) In a small saucepan, bring the cranberries to a boil to soften, then transfer to a small mixing bowl and let cool.

3) In a stand mixer with a paddle attachment, cream together the butter and sugar until the mixture is light and fluffy. Once finished, add eggs one at a time and beat until thoroughly incorporated, scraping down the sides of the bowl after each egg. Add the vanilla extract, followed by the Greek yogurt.

4) In a separate medium mixing bowl, combine flour, baking powder, baking soda, salt and cinnamon. Add the flour mixture to the butter/sugar/egg mixture, mixing briefly, just enough to incorporate all ingredients.

5) Add the cooled cranberry mixture to the batter, using a rubber spatula to incorporate. This will help avoid over-mixing!

6) Transfer mixture to the prepared Bundt pan and spread batter evenly throughout the pan. Bake at 350 for 50–55 minutes or until a toothpick comes out mostly clean.

7) Allow the cake to rest in the pan for up to 30 minutes, then turn out of the pan and allow to completely cool on a wire cooling rack.

8) Top with Cinnamon Glaze (page 201) and serve.

—CHOCOLATE CAKE—

TIME: 60 MINUTES   SERVES: 8–10

Chocolate cake is a classic for a reason. Baking a chocolate cake in a Bundt pan is a surefire way to ensure the most beautiful cake your guests have ever seen. Pair this recipe with any of the options in the Glazes, Sauces, and Frostings (page 186) section for a guaranteed success!

3/4 CUP BUTTER, ROOM TEMPERATURE

1 1/3 CUPS SUGAR

2 EGGS, ROOM TEMPERATURE

1 CUP BUTTERMILK

1 TEASPOON VANILLA EXTRACT

1 3/4 CUPS ALL-PURPOSE FLOUR

2/3 CUP DUTCH-PROCESSED COCOA POWDER

1/2 TEASPOON SALT

2 TEASPOONS BAKING SODA

CHOCOLATE GLAZE (PAGE 191)

CHOPPED PISTACHIOS, IF DESIRED

1) Preheat oven to 350 degrees. Liberally coat the Bundt pan with butter or canola oil spray and lightly flour, tapping out the excess flour to create a thin, even coat.

2) In a stand mixer with a paddle attachment, cream together the butter and sugar until the mixture is light and fluffy. Once finished, add the eggs one at a time and beat until thoroughly incorporated, scraping down the sides of the bowl after each egg. Add vanilla extract.

3) In a separate medium mixing bowl, combine flour, cocoa powder, baking soda, and salt.

4) Add 1/3 of the flour mixture to the stand mixer bowl with the butter-sugar mixture. Then add 1/3 of the buttermilk to the stand mixer bowl. Repeat this process, alternating between adding dry ingredients and buttermilk.

5) Transfer the cake batter mixture to the prepared Bundt pan and spread batter evenly throughout the pan.

6) Bake at 350 for 45–50 minutes, or until a toothpick comes out mostly clean.

7) Allow the cake to rest in the pan for up to 30 minutes, then turn out of the pan and allow to completely cool on a wire cooling rack.

8) Once cooled, top with Chocolate Glaze (page 191) and chopped pistachios, if desired.

—GLUTEN-FREE CHOCOLATE CAKE—

TIME: 60 MINUTES   SERVES: 8–10

This gluten-free chocolate cake is the perfect base for many of the recipes in this book. Experiment with different glazes or additions to this staple recipe.

3/4 CUP BUTTER, ROOM TEMPERATURE

1 1/3 CUPS SUGAR

2 EGGS, ROOM TEMPERATURE

1 CUP BUTTERMILK

1 TEASPOON VANILLA EXTRACT

2 CUPS GLUTEN-FREE FLOUR

1 TEASPOON XANTHAN GUM

2/3 CUP DUTCH-PROCESSED COCOA POWDER

1/2 TEASPOON SALT

2 TEASPOONS BAKING SODA

1) Preheat oven to 350 degrees. Liberally coat the Bundt pan with butter or canola oil spray and lightly flour, tapping out the excess flour to create a thin, even coat.

2) In a stand mixer with a paddle attachment, cream together the butter and sugar until the mixture is light and fluffy. Once finished, add the eggs one at a time and beat until thoroughly incorporated, scraping down the sides of the bowl after each egg. Add vanilla extract.

3) In a separate medium mixing bowl, combine flour, cocoa powder, baking soda, and salt.

4) Add ⅓ of the flour mixture to the stand mixer bowl with the butter-sugar mixture. Then add ⅓ of the buttermilk to the stand mixer bowl. Repeat this process, alternating between adding dry ingredients and buttermilk.

5) Transfer the cake batter mixture to the prepared Bundt pan and spread batter evenly throughout the pan.

6) Bake at 350 for 45–50 minutes, or until a toothpick comes out mostly clean.

7) Allow the cake to rest in the pan for up to 30 minutes, then turn out of the pan and allow to completely cool on a wire cooling rack.

8) Once cooled, dust with powdered sugar using a fine meshed sieve.

—CHOCOLATE ALMOND CAKE—

TIME: 60 MINUTES   SERVES: 8–10

Some days require an extra dose of decadence. Some days are just Wednesdays. In either case, enjoy your afternoon coffee with a slab of toasted chocolate nuttiness, and remember it's always okay to treat yourself.

¾ CUP BUTTER, ROOM TEMPERATURE

1 ⅓ CUPS SUGAR

2 EGGS, ROOM TEMPERATURE

1 CUP BUTTERMILK

1 TEASPOON VANILLA EXTRACT

1 TEASPOON ALMOND EXTRACT

1 ¾ CUPS ALL-PURPOSE FLOUR

⅔ CUP DUTCH-PROCESSED COCOA POWDER

½ TEASPOON SALT

2 TEASPOONS BAKING SODA

1 CUP SLICED ALMONDS, TOASTED

CHOCOLATE GLAZE (PAGE 191)

1) Preheat oven to 350 degrees. Liberally coat the Bundt pan with butter or canola oil spray and lightly flour, tapping out the excess flour to create a thin, even coat.

2) In a stand mixer with a paddle attachment, cream together the butter and sugar until the mixture is light and fluffy. Once finished, add the eggs one at a time and beat until thoroughly incorporated, scraping down the sides of the bowl after each egg. Add vanilla and almond extracts.

3) In a separate medium mixing bowl, combine flour, cocoa powder, baking soda, and salt.

4) Add ⅓ of the flour mixture to the stand mixer bowl with the butter-sugar mixture. Then add ⅓ of the buttermilk to the stand mixer bowl. Repeat this process, alternating between adding dry ingredients and buttermilk.

5) In a medium, dry skillet over medium heat, add sliced almonds, stirring occasionally for 3 minutes or until fragrant and lightly toasted.

6) Spread the toasted almond slices into the bottom of the prepared Bundt pan. Transfer the cake batter mixture to the prepared Bundt pan and spread batter evenly throughout the pan.

7) Bake at 350 for 45–50 minutes, or until a toothpick comes out mostly clean.

8) Allow the cake to rest in the pan for up to 30 minutes, then turn out of the pan and allow to completely cool on a wire cooling rack.

9) Once cooled, top with Chocolate Glaze (page 191).

—MEXICAN CHOCOLATE CAKE—

TIME: 80 MINUTES   SERVES: 8–10

Sticky buns, eat your heart out. This classic combination of chocolate and cinnamon proves that the spice deserves a starring role in more desserts.

1 CUP BUTTER, ROOM TEMPERATURE

2 CUPS SUGAR

2 EGGS, ROOM TEMPERATURE

½ CUP BUTTERMILK

2 TABLESPOONS VANILLA EXTRACT

2 CUPS ALL-PURPOSE FLOUR

½ CUP DUTCH-PROCESSED COCOA POWDER

1 TEASPOON BAKING SODA

½ TEASPOON CINNAMON

¼ TEASPOON SALT

CINNAMON GLAZE (PAGE 201)

1) Preheat oven to 350 degrees. Liberally coat the Bundt pan with butter or canola oil spray and lightly flour, tapping out the excess flour to create a thin, even coat.

2) In a stand mixer with a paddle attachment, cream together the butter and sugar until the mixture is light and fluffy. Once finished, add the eggs one at a time and beat until thoroughly incorporated, scraping down the sides of the bowl after each egg. Add vanilla extract.

3) In a separate medium-sized mixing bowl, combine flour, cocoa powder, baking soda, cinnamon and salt.

4) Add ⅓ of the flour mixture to the stand mixer bowl with the butter-sugar mixture. Add ⅓ of the buttermilk to the stand mixer bowl. Repeat this process, alternating between adding dry ingredients and buttermilk.

5) Transfer cake batter mixture to the prepared Bundt pan and spread batter evenly throughout the pan.

6) Bake at 350 for 50–55 minutes, or until a toothpick comes out mostly clean.

7) Allow the cake to rest in the pan for up to 30 minutes, then turn out of the pan and allow to completely cool on a wire cooling rack. Top with Cinnamon Glaze (page 201) or marble together with Chocolate Glaze (page 191) before serving.

—CHERRY CHOCOLATE CAKE—

TIME: 70 MINUTES   SERVES: 8–10

Few things are as compatible as tart, deep red, summer cherries and dark, slightly bitter chocolate. We love Ghirardelli 60% cacao dark chocolate chips in this recipe, but feel free to use your personal favorite. Note: Milk chocolate will make this cake significantly sweeter, so feel free to reduce the amount of granulated sugar, or don't and indulge your sweet tooth!

½ CUP BUTTER, ROOM TEMPERATURE

½ CUP SUGAR

2 EGGS, ROOM TEMPERATURE

1 TEASPOON VANILLA EXTRACT

1 CUP GREEK YOGURT

2 ½ CUPS ALL-PURPOSE FLOUR

½ TEASPOON BAKING SODA

1 TEASPOON BAKING POWDER

½ TEASPOON SALT

2 CUPS DARK CHOCOLATE CHUNKS

2 CUPS CHERRIES, PITTED AND CHOPPED

1) Preheat the oven to 350 degrees. Liberally coat the Bundt pan with butter or canola oil spray and lightly flour, tapping out the excess flour to create a thin, even coat.

2) Rinse the cherries thoroughly, then use a cherry pitter or pairing knife to remove their pits and roughly chop them. Set aside.

3) In a stand mixer with a paddle attachment, cream together the butter and sugar until light and fluffy. Once finished, add the eggs one at a time and beat until thoroughly incorporated, scraping down the sides of the bowls after each egg. Add vanilla extract and yogurt.

4) In a separate bowl, mix together all-purpose flour, baking powder, baking soda and salt. Add the flour mixture to olive butter/sugar/egg mixture, mixing just until incorporated. Gently mix in the cherries and chocolate.

5) Transfer cake batter to your prepared Bundt pan. Bake at 350 for 45-50 minutes, or until a toothpick comes out mostly clean.

6) Remove from heat. Let the cake to rest in the pan for up to 30 minutes, then turn out of the pan and allow to completely cool on a wire cooling rack.

—CHOCOLATE MINT CAKE—

TIME: 60 MINUTES   SERVES: 8–10

This minty cake is sure to be an instant holiday classic. Play up the beautiful ring by decorating with mint candies and drizzled chocolate, or even decorate like a wreath to use this cake as a holiday centerpiece.

3/4 CUP BUTTER, ROOM TEMPERATURE

1 1/3 CUPS SUGAR

2 EGGS, ROOM TEMPERATURE

1 CUP BUTTERMILK

1 TEASPOON VANILLA EXTRACT

1 TEASPOON PEPPERMINT EXTRACT

1 3/4 CUPS ALL-PURPOSE FLOUR

2/3 CUP DUTCH-PROCESSED COCOA POWDER

1/2 TEASPOON SALT

2 TEASPOONS BAKING SODA

PEPPERMINT GLAZE (PAGE 195)

CRUSHED PEPPERMINT CANDY, FOR GARNISH

1) Preheat oven to 350 degrees. Liberally coat the Bundt pan with butter or canola oil spray and lightly flour, tapping out the excess flour to create a thin, even coat.

2) In a stand mixer with a paddle attachment, cream together the butter and sugar until the mixture is light and fluffy. Once finished, add the eggs one at a time and beat until thoroughly incorporated, scraping down the sides of the bowl after each egg. Add vanilla and peppermint extracts.

3) In a separate medium mixing bowl, combine flour, cocoa powder, baking soda, and salt.

4) Add ⅓ of the flour mixture to the stand mixer bowl with the butter-sugar mixture. Then add ⅓ of the buttermilk to the stand mixer bowl. Repeat this process, alternating between adding dry ingredients and buttermilk.

5) Transfer the cake batter mixture to the prepared Bundt pan and spread batter evenly throughout the pan.

6) Bake at 350 for 45–50 minutes, or until a toothpick comes out mostly clean.

7) Allow the cake to rest in the pan for up to 30 minutes, then turn out of the pan and allow to completely cool on a wire cooling rack.

8) Once cooled, dust with powdered sugar using a fine meshed sieve.

9) Top with Peppermint Glaze (page 195) and peppermint candies.

—CHOCOLATE CARAMEL CAKE—

TIME: 60 MINUTES   SERVES: 8–10

Gooey caramel makes this cake irresistible, and the chocolate and caramel combination adds an extra level of sinful. Serve warm with ice cream for a true triple threat.

3/4 CUP BUTTER, ROOM TEMPERATURE

1 1/3 CUPS SUGAR

2 EGGS, ROOM TEMPERATURE

1 CUP BUTTERMILK

1 TEASPOON VANILLA EXTRACT

1 TEASPOON PEPPERMINT EXTRACT

1 3/4 CUPS ALL-PURPOSE FLOUR

2/3 CUP DUTCH-PROCESSED COCOA POWDER

1/2 TEASPOON SALT

2 TEASPOONS BAKING SODA

CARAMEL SAUCE (PAGE 202)

1) Preheat oven to 350 degrees. Liberally coat the Bundt pan with butter or canola oil spray and lightly flour, tapping out the excess flour to create a thin, even coat.

2) In a stand mixer with a paddle attachment, cream together the butter and sugar until the mixture is light and fluffy. Once finished, add the eggs one at a time and beat until thoroughly incorporated, scraping down the sides of the bowl after each egg. Add vanilla extract.

3) In a separate medium mixing bowl, combine flour, cocoa powder, baking soda, and salt.

4) Add 1/3 of the flour mixture to the stand mixer bowl with the butter-sugar mixture. Then add 1/3 of the buttermilk to the stand mixer bowl. Repeat this process, alternating between adding dry ingredients and buttermilk.

5) Transfer the cake batter mixture to the prepared Bundt pan and spread batter evenly throughout the pan.

6) Bake at 350 for 45–50 minutes, or until a toothpick comes out mostly clean.

7) Allow the cake to rest in the pan for up to 30 minutes, then turn out of the pan and allow to completely cool on a wire cooling rack.

8) Once cooled, top with Caramel Sauce (page 202).

-ROCKY ROAD CAKE-

TIME: 60 MINUTES   SERVES: 8–10

An ice cream favorite is the inspiration for this delicious dessert. The nuts and marshmallows make for a beautifully complex cake.

¾ CUP BUTTER, ROOM TEMPERATURE

1 ⅓ CUPS SUGAR

2 EGGS, ROOM TEMPERATURE

1 CUP BUTTERMILK

1 TEASPOON VANILLA EXTRACT

1 ¾ CUPS ALL-PURPOSE FLOUR

⅔ CUP DUTCH-PROCESSED COCOA POWDER

½ TEASPOON SALT

2 TEASPOONS BAKING SODA

½ CUP MINIATURE MARSHMALLOWS

½ CUP WALNUTS, CHOPPED

CHOCOLATE GLAZE (PAGE 191), IF DESIRED.

1) Preheat oven to 350 degrees. Liberally coat the Bundt pan with butter or canola oil spray and lightly flour, tapping out the excess flour to create a thin, even coat.

2) In a stand mixer with a paddle attachment, cream together the butter and sugar until the mixture is light and fluffy. Once finished, add the eggs one at a time and beat until thoroughly incorporated, scraping down the sides of the bowl after each egg. Add vanilla extract.

3) In a separate medium mixing bowl, combine flour, cocoa powder, baking soda, and salt.

4) Add ⅓ of the flour mixture to the stand mixer bowl with the butter-sugar mixture. Then add ⅓ of the buttermilk to the stand mixer bowl. Repeat this process, alternating between adding dry ingredients and buttermilk.

5) Add the marshmallows and walnuts, and stir until just combined.

6) Transfer the cake batter mixture to the prepared Bundt pan and spread batter evenly throughout the pan.

7) Bake at 350 for 45-50 minutes, or until a toothpick comes out mostly clean.

8) Allow the cake to rest in the pan for up to 30 minutes, then turn out of the pan and allow to completely cool on a wire cooling rack. Drizzle on Chocolate Glaze (page 191), if desired.

—PINEAPPLE UPSIDE DOWN CAKE—

TIME: 70 MINUTES   SERVES: 8–10

This classic recipe is only made better by baking it in a Bundt. This decadent ring is sure to be a hit!

1/4 CUP BUTTER, MELTED

1/2 CUP BROWN SUGAR

6 -8 PINEAPPLE RINGS

1/4 CUP MARASCHINO
CHERRIES, CHOPPED

3/4 CUP BUTTER, ROOM
TEMPERATURE

1 1/3 CUPS SUGAR

3 EGGS, ROOM
TEMPERATURE

1 TABLESPOON VANILLA
EXTRACT

3/4 CUP BUTTERMILK

2 CUPS ALL-PURPOSE
FLOUR

1/2 TEASPOON BAKING SODA

1 TEASPOON BAKING
POWDER

1 TEASPOON SALT

1/2 TEASPOON CINNAMON

1) Preheat oven to 350 degrees. Liberally coat the Bundt pan with butter or canola oil spray and lightly flour, tapping out the excess flour to create a thin, even coat.

2) Spread melted butter over the bottom of the pan. Sprinkle brown sugar over the melted butter. Place the pineapple slices in concentric circles in the brown sugar mixture. Place the cherries throughout.

3) In a stand mixer with a paddle attachment, cream together the butter and sugar until the mixture is light and fluffy. Once finished, add the eggs one at a time and beat until thoroughly incorporated, scraping down the sides of the bowl after each egg. Add vanilla extract.

4) In a separate medium mixing bowl, combine flour, baking soda, baking powder, salt, and cinnamon.

5) Add 1/3 of the flour mixture to the stand mixer bowl with the butter/sugar mixture. Then add 1/3 of the buttermilk to the stand mixer bowl. Repeat this process, alternating between adding dry ingredients and buttermilk.

6) Transfer cake batter mixture to the prepared Bundt pan and spread batter evenly throughout the pan, on top of the brown sugar and pineapple. Bake at 350 for 45-50 minutes or until a toothpick comes out mostly clean.

7) Allow the cake to rest in the pan for up to 20 minutes or when the pan is still warm to the touch, then turn out of the pan and allow to completely cool on a wire cooling rack. Note: This one needs to be a little warmer when you remove it from the pan to ensure that the pineapple and brown sugar mixture come out intact.

—MAPLE CINNAMON APPLE UPSIDE DOWN CAKE—

TIME: 70 MINUTES   SERVES: 8–10

This crumbly butter cake, built and baked upside down, is sure to fill your house with a heavenly apple-and-syrup aroma. Serve it with crème fraîche for extra fancy points!

1 CUP MAPLE SYRUP

1 TEASPOON SALT

1 1/2 CUPS GRANNY SMITH APPLES, CORED, PEELED AND CUT INTO 1/4-INCH SLICES

3/4 CUP BUTTER, ROOM TEMPERATURE

1 1/3 CUPS SUGAR

3 EGGS, ROOM TEMPERATURE

1 TABLESPOON VANILLA EXTRACT

3/4 CUP BUTTERMILK

2 CUPS ALL-PURPOSE FLOUR

1/2 TEASPOON BAKING SODA

1 TEASPOON BAKING POWDER

1 TEASPOON SALT

1/2 TEASPOON CINNAMON

1) Preheat oven to 350 degrees. Liberally coat the Bundt pan with butter or canola oil spray and lightly flour, tapping out the excess flour to create a thin, even coat.

2) In a small saucepan over medium heat, combine maple syrup and salt together until it achieves a thinner consistency. Pour evenly into the bottom of the prepared Bundt pan.

3) Place the apple slices in concentric circles in the maple syrup mixture.

4) In a stand mixer with a paddle attachment, cream together the butter and sugar until the mixture is light and fluffy. Once finished, add the eggs one at a time and beat until thoroughly incorporated, scraping down the sides of the bowl after each egg. Add vanilla extract.

5) In a separate medium mixing bowl, combine flour, baking soda, baking powder, salt, and cinnamon.

6) Add 1/3 of the flour mixture to the stand mixer bowl with the butter/sugar mixture. Then add 1/3 of the buttermilk to the stand mixer bowl. Repeat this process, alternating between adding dry ingredients and buttermilk.

7) Transfer cake batter mixture to the prepared Bundt pan and spread batter evenly throughout the pan, on top of the maple syrup and apples. Bake at 350 for 45–50 minutes or until a toothpick comes out mostly clean.

8) Allow the cake to rest in the pan for up to 20 minutes or when the pan is still warm to the touch, then turn out of the pan and allow to completely cool on a wire cooling rack. Note: This one needs to be a little warmer when you remove it from the pan to ensure that the apples and maple syrup mixture come out intact.

—PECAN PEAR UPSIDE DOWN CAKE—

TIME: 70 MINUTES   SERVES: 8–10

This delicious upside down cake features some fresh flavors that are sure to impress your family or dinner guests.

1/4 CUP BUTTER, MELTED

1/2 CUP BROWN SUGAR

2 PEARS, QUARTERED

1/4 CUP PECANS, CHOPPED

3/4 CUP BUTTER, ROOM TEMPERATURE

1 1/3 CUPS SUGAR

3 EGGS, ROOM TEMPERATURE

1 TABLESPOON VANILLA EXTRACT

3/4 CUP BUTTERMILK

2 CUPS ALL-PURPOSE FLOUR

1/2 TEASPOON BAKING SODA

1 TEASPOON BAKING POWDER

1 TEASPOON SALT

1/2 TEASPOON CINNAMON

1) Preheat oven to 350 degrees. Liberally coat the Bundt pan with butter or canola oil spray and lightly flour, tapping out the excess flour to create a thin, even coat.

2) Spread melted butter over the bottom of the pan. Sprinkle brown sugar over the melted butter.

3) Place the pears in the brown sugar mixture. Place the pecans throughout.

4) In a stand mixer with a paddle attachment, cream together the butter and sugar until the mixture is light and fluffy. Once finished, add the eggs one at a time and beat until thoroughly incorporated, scraping down the sides of the bowl after each egg. Add vanilla extract.

5) In a separate medium mixing bowl, combine flour, baking soda, baking powder, salt, and cinnamon.

6) Add 1/3 of the flour mixture to the stand mixer bowl with the butter/sugar mixture. Then add 1/3 of the buttermilk to the stand mixer bowl. Repeat this process, alternating between adding dry ingredients and buttermilk.

7) Transfer cake batter mixture to the prepared Bundt pan and spread batter evenly throughout the pan, on top of the brown sugar and pears. Bake at 350 for 45-50 minutes or until a toothpick comes out mostly clean.

8) Allow the cake to rest in the pan for up to 20 minutes or when the pan is still warm to the touch, then turn out of the pan and allow to completely cool on a wire cooling rack. Note: This one needs to be a little warmer when you remove it from the pan to ensure that the pear and brown sugar mixture come out intact.

—SPICE CAKE—

TIME: 70 MINUTES   SERVES: 8–10

A classic and delicious array of spices is certain to please any taste bud. This cake has a lot of taste on its own, so opt for a simpler glaze like cream cheese or vanilla to balance out the flavors.

1 CUP BUTTER, ROOM TEMPERATURE

2 ½ CUPS SUGAR

3 EGGS, ROOM TEMPERATURE

3 CUPS ALL-PURPOSE FLOUR

2 TEASPOONS BAKING SODA

1½ TEASPOONS GROUND GINGER

1 TEASPOON CINNAMON

1 TEASPOON NUTMEG

¼ TEASPOON CLOVES

½ TEASPOON SALT

½ CUP RAISINS

1) Preheat oven to 350 degrees. Liberally coat the Bundt pan with butter or canola oil spray and lightly flour, tapping out the excess flour to create a thin, even coat.

2) In a stand mixer with a paddle attachment, cream together the butter and sugar until the mixture is light and fluffy. Once finished, add eggs one at a time and beat until thoroughly incorporated, scraping down the sides of the bowl after each egg. Add the carrots.

3) In a separate medium mixing bowl, combine the flour, baking soda, ginger, cinnamon, nutmeg, cloves and salt. Add the flour and spice mixture to the egg mixture and mix briefly—just enough to incorporate all the ingredients.

4) Add raisins and mix until just combined.

5) Transfer the mixture to your prepared Bundt pan and spread batter evenly throughout the pan. Bake at 350 for 45-50 minutes or until a toothpick comes out mostly clean.

6) Allow the cake to rest in the pan for up to 30 minutes, then turn out of the pan and allow to completely cool on a wire cooling rack. Top with Cream Cheese Glaze (page 191) before serving.

—PUMPKIN SPICE CAKE WITH TOASTED PECANS—

TIME: 70 MINUTES   SERVES: 8–10

This cake is a showstopper at Thanksgiving dinner, and the leftovers (if there are any) will go great with your morning coffee.

1 CUP PECANS, ROUGHLY CHOPPED

1 CUP BUTTER, ROOM TEMPERATURE

2 1/2 CUPS SUGAR

3 EGGS, ROOM TEMPERATURE

15 OUNCES (1 SMALL CAN) CANNED PUMPKIN PUREE

3 CUPS ALL-PURPOSE FLOUR

2 TEASPOONS BAKING SODA

1 TEASPOON CINNAMON

1 TEASPOON NUTMEG

1/4 TEASPOON CLOVES

1/2 TEASPOON SALT

1) Preheat oven to 350 degrees. Liberally coat the Bundt pan with butter or canola oil spray and lightly flour, tapping out the excess flour to create a thin, even coat.

2) Add chopped pecans to a medium, dry skillet over medium heat, stirring occasionally for 3 minutes or until the pecans are lightly toasted and fragrant.

3) Transfer toasted pecans to the bottom of the prepared Bundt pan.

4) In a stand mixer with a paddle attachment, cream together the butter and sugar until the mixture is light and fluffy. Once finished, add eggs one at a time and beat until thoroughly incorporated, scraping down the sides of the bowl after each egg. Add the pumpkin puree.

5) In a separate medium mixing bowl, combine the flour, baking soda, cinnamon, nutmeg, cloves and salt. Add the flour and spice mixture to the egg mixture and mix briefly—just enough to incorporate all the ingredients.

6) Transfer the mixture to your prepared Bundt pan and spread batter evenly throughout the pan. Bake at 350 for 45-50 minutes or until a toothpick comes out mostly clean.

7) Allow the cake to rest in the pan for up to 30 minutes, then turn out of the pan and allow to completely cool on a wire cooling rack.

—RED VELVET CAKE—

TIME: 80 MINUTES   SERVES: 8–10

Though a Christmas favorite to be sure, this not-too-sweet but oh-so-gorgeous cake can still be made whenever the mood strikes. Shower with powdered sugar and cocoa powder or make the Cream Cheese Glaze (page 191) for extra richness.

1 CUP BUTTER, ROOM TEMPERATURE

1 ½ CUPS SUGAR

2 EGGS, ROOM TEMPERATURE

1 CUP BUTTERMILK

2 TABLESPOONS RED FOOD COLORING

1 TEASPOON WHITE VINEGAR

1 TEASPOON VANILLA EXTRACT

2 ½ CUPS ALL-PURPOSE FLOUR

1 TEASPOON BAKING SODA

1 TEASPOON SALT

1 TEASPOON COCOA POWDER

CREAM CHEESE GLAZE (PAGE 191)

1) Preheat oven to 350 degrees. Liberally coat the Bundt pan with butter or canola oil spray and lightly flour, tapping out the excess flour to create a thin, even coat.

2) In a stand mixer with a paddle attachment, cream together the butter and sugar until the mixture is light and fluffy. Once finished, add the eggs one at a time and beat until thoroughly incorporated, scraping down the sides of the bowl after each egg. Add red food coloring, white vinegar and vanilla extract.

3) In a separate medium mixing bowl, combine flour, baking soda, salt and cocoa powder.

4) Add ⅓ of the flour mixture to the stand mixer bowl with the butter-sugar mixture. Then add ⅓ of the buttermilk to the stand mixer bowl. Repeat this process, alternating between adding dry ingredients and buttermilk.

5) Transfer mixture to the prepared Bundt pan and spread batter evenly throughout the pan.

6) Bake at 350 for 45–50 minutes, or until a toothpick comes out mostly clean.

7) Let the cake to rest in the pan for up to 30 minutes, then turn out of the pan and allow to completely cool on a wire cooling rack.

—CARROT CAKE—

The Carrot Cake is that classic treat that everyone can enjoy without feeling guilty.

1 CUP PECANS, ROUGHLY CHOPPED

1 CUP BUTTER, ROOM TEMPERATURE

2 ½ CUPS SUGAR

3 EGGS, ROOM TEMPERATURE

2 CUPS GRATED CARROTS

3 CUPS ALL-PURPOSE FLOUR

2 TEASPOONS BAKING SODA

1 TEASPOON CINNAMON

1 TEASPOON NUTMEG

¼ TEASPOON CLOVES

½ TEASPOON SALT

CREAM CHEESE GLAZE (PAGE 191)

1) Preheat oven to 350 degrees. Liberally coat the Bundt pan with butter or canola oil spray and lightly flour, tapping out the excess flour to create a thin, even coat.

2) Add chopped pecans to a medium, dry skillet over medium heat, stirring occasionally for 3 minutes or until the pecans are lightly toasted and fragrant.

3) Transfer toasted pecans to the bottom of the prepared Bundt pan.

4) In a stand mixer with a paddle attachment, cream together the butter and sugar until the mixture is light and fluffy. Once finished, add eggs one at a time and beat until thoroughly incorporated, scraping down the sides of the bowl after each egg. Add the carrots.

5) In a separate medium mixing bowl, combine the flour, baking soda, cinnamon, nutmeg, cloves and salt. Add the flour and spice mixture to the egg mixture and mix briefly—just enough to incorporate all the ingredients.

6) Transfer the mixture to your prepared Bundt pan and spread batter evenly throughout the pan. Bake at 350 for 45-50 minutes or until a toothpick comes out mostly clean.

7) Allow the cake to rest in the pan for up to 30 minutes, then turn out of the pan and allow to completely cool on a wire cooling rack. Top with Cream Cheese Glaze (page 191) before serving.

Innovative Ideas:

MOLTEN CENTER

For the simplest molten cake ever, use the Bundt's center hole as a sauce vessel. After plating, fill the middle opening with caramel, chocolate sauce, whipped cream, or any other filling. The first slice will make the cake's gooey center explode. Try this trick with mini Bundt cakes for personal molten treats.

PEELING STAND

Corn cobs, carrots, zucchinis—if it's wide enough, it can be peeled easily into a Bundt pan. Just stand your vegetable longways and, using the center circle as a base, peel in a downward motion into your Bundt pan. It's a nifty trick that guarantees knife safety, and you don't need to clean off the cutting board after you're done.

FRUIT BASKET

If you don't want to get fancy with your centerpiece, try using your Bundt as a fruit bowl. Not only does it still work as a table display, but it's quite practical too. Just pick out your handsomest Bundt, add whatever favorites you like to keep on hand and enjoy.

Glazes, Sauces, and Frostings

No cake is complete without a topping! The sugary glazes are perfect to drizzle over any Bundt cake as a finishing touch. The frostings make decorating with style incredibly simple. The sauces can take any treat to the next level. Mix and match any of these toppings with any of the recipes in this book to try out new, fun flavor combinations. Or, use these recipes on their own. The glazes are great on breads; the frostings work with any cake; and the sauces are a perfect ice cream sundae addition. Try using the Confectioner's Sugar Glaze (page 188) with your favorite flavor extract to create your own combination, like almond, maple, anise, or any other extract you enjoy!

-CONFECTIONER'S SUGAR GLAZE-

TIME: 5 MINUTES

This easy glaze dresses up any bread or cake, and hardens in less than an hour.

4 CUPS CONFECTIONER'S SUGAR

4-5 TABLESPOONS WATER

½ TEASPOON VANILLA EXTRACT

1) Combine confectioner's sugar, water, and vanilla in a mixing bowl, adding additional water if too thick.

2) Use a whisk or spoon to drizzle the glaze over cooled cake.

-VANILLA GLAZE-

TIME: 5 MINUTES

This simple, delicious glaze goes well with just about any cake.

1 CUP POWDERED SUGAR

2 TABLESPOONS WHOLE MILK

1 TEASPOON VANILLA EXTRACT

1) Whisk together the powdered sugar, milk, and vanilla extract.

2) Use a whisk to drizzle the glaze over cooled cake.

This recipe is a great base **FOR ALL OTHER GLAZES.**

SUBSTITUTE ANY FRUIT JUICE FOR THE WATER OR OTHER EXTRACTS FOR THE VANILLA FOR AN ENTIRELY DIFFERENT FLAVOR.

—CREAM CHEESE GLAZE—

TIME: 10 MINUTES

The *ultimate* topping for Red Velvet and Carrot cakes, this versatile favorite
is a tasty addition to any cake.

**1 CUP CREAM CHEESE,
ROOM TEMPERATURE**

2 CUPS POWDERED SUGAR

**2-4 TABLESPOONS WHOLE
MILK, ROOM TEMPERATURE**

1) Stir together cream cheese, powdered sugar and milk
(1 tablespoon at a time) in a mixing bowl. The finished
product should have a thick, glue-like consistency.

2) Use a whisk to drizzle the Cream Cheese Glaze onto the
cooled cake.

—CHOCOLATE GLAZE—

TIME: 10 MINUTES

Because chocolate makes everything better.

**2 CUPS CONFECTIONERS'
SUGAR**

**1/2 CUP UNSWEETENED
COCOA POWDER**

**1/2 TEASPOON PURE
VANILLA EXTRACT**

1/4 CUP MILK

1) Sift confectioners' sugar and cocoa into a mixing bowl.

2) Add vanilla and all but 1 tablespoon milk, and whisk
well until smooth. Add remaining milk if too thick to use
as a glaze.

**THE ICING CAN BE KEPT REFRIGERATED
IN AN AIRTIGHT CONTAINER FOR UP TO 5
DAYS. BRING IT TO ROOM TEMPERATURE
BEFORE USING.**

**FOR MOCHA GLAZE, BRING THE MILK TO
A BOIL AND DISSOLVE 1 TABLESPOON
INSTANT ESPRESSO POWDER IN IT.**

—CHOCOLATE GANACHE—

This rich Chocolate Ganache is great for adding a little decadence to your dessert.
We love it on Banana Bread!

1 CUP HEAVY CREAM

1 ¾ CUPS DARK CHOCOLATE CHIPS

1) In a small saucepan, boil the heavy cream. Keep a close eye on it—if left too long, it will boil over and taste burnt.

2) Add the chocolate chips to a medium mixing bowl. Pour the hot heavy cream over the chocolate chips and stir until blended evenly.

3) Drizzle over cooled cake.

—CHOCOLATE PEPPERMINT GANACHE—

TIME: 10 MINUTES

A richer alternative to our Peppermint Glaze, this topping will make sure your bundt
is the star of any holiday party!

1 CUP HEAVY CREAM

1 ¾ CUPS DARK CHOCOLATE CHIPS

1 TEASPOON PURE PEPPERMINT EXTRACT, ADD MORE TO TASTE IF DESIRED

CRUSHED CANDY CANES OR PEPPERMINTS (OPTIONAL)

1) In a small saucepan, boil the heavy cream. Keep a close eye on it and make sure it doesn't boil over.

2) Add the chocolate chips and peppermint extract to a medium mixing bowl. Pour the hot heavy cream over the chocolate chips and stir until blended evenly.

3) Drizzle over cooled cake and top with crushed candy cane pieces, if desired.

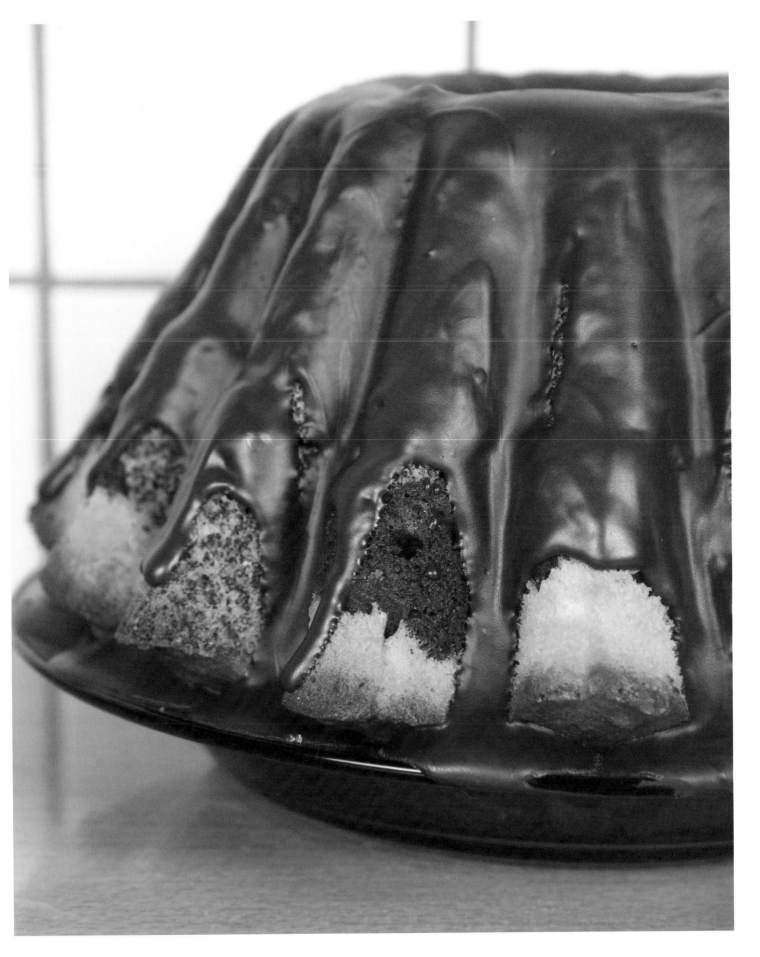

—PEPPERMINT GLAZE—

This cool Peppermint Glaze adds a festive touch to wintertime treats.

1 CUP POWDERED SUGAR

2 TABLESPOONS WHOLE MILK

1 TEASPOON PEPPERMINT EXTRACT, MORE TO TASTE

1 TEASPOON VANILLA EXTRACT (OPTIONAL)

CRUSHED CANDY CANE PIECES OR PEPPERMINTS (OPTIONAL)

1) Whisk together the powdered sugar, milk, and peppermint extract.

2) Use a whisk to drizzle the glaze over cooled cake.

3) Top with crushed candy cane pieces, if desired.

—LEMON GLAZE—

TIME: 5 MINUTES

A classic Bundt cake topping, this lemony confection will have you reaching for one more slice!

1 CUP POWDERED SUGAR

LEMON JUICE FROM ½ A LEMON

1 TABLESPOON LEMON ZEST (OPTIONAL)

1) Stir together powdered sugar, lemon juice and lemon zest (if desired) in a mixing bowl.

2) Use a whisk to drizzle the Lemon Glaze on the cooled cake.

—ORANGE ZEST GLAZE—

TIME: 5 MINUTES

The bright citrus flavors of this Orange Zest Glaze are a versatile addition to any cake!

1 CUP POWDERED SUGAR

2 TABLESPOONS MILK

1 TABLESPOON FRESH ORANGE JUICE

1 TABLESPOON ORANGE ZEST

1) Whisk together powdered sugar, milk, orange juice and orange zest.

2) Use a whisk to drizzle glaze over cooled cake.

–STRAWBERRY GLAZE–

TIME: 10 MINUTES

Perfect for summer cakes and fantastic with a side of whipped cream and fresh berries.

1 CUP POWDERED SUGAR

1/2 CUP MINCED OR BLENDED STRAWBERRIES

1-2 TABLESPOONS WATER

1/2 TEASPOON LEMON JUICE (OPTIONAL)

1) Stir together powdered sugar, strawberries, water and lemon juice (if desired) in a mixing bowl.

2) Use a whisk to drizzle the glaze over cooled cake.

–CARAMEL GLAZE–

TIME: 20 MINUTES

Sticky, sweet, and guaranteed to have you coming back for more, this Caramel Glaze is a game-changer!

1/2 CUP EVAPORATED MILK

1/2 CUP BROWN SUGAR

1 EGG YOLK

4 TABLESPOONS (1/4 CUP) BUTTER, CUT INTO SLICES

1/2 TEASPOON VANILLA EXTRACT

1/4 TEASPOON SALT

1) In a large saucepan, combine the evaporated milk, sugar, egg yolk, butter, and vanilla.

2) Cook over medium heat, stirring frequently, until thickened and golden, about 10 to 12 minutes.

3) Take off the stove and allow to cool, stirring occasionally.

4) Spread or pour over the top of cooled cake.

—CINNAMON GLAZE—

This Cinnamon Glaze lends the perfect touch of spice to Mexican Chocolate Cake.

¼ CUP POWDERED SUGAR

1 TABLESPOON WHOLE MILK, MORE AS REQUIRED

½ TEASPOON CINNAMON

1) Whisk together powdered sugar, whole milk and cinnamon. Add more whole milk or powdered sugar to get a glue-like consistency.

2) Drizzle over cooled cake, holding a whisk about 6 inches above the cake. Move the whisk in a back and forth motion to create thin stripes.

—VANILLA BUTTERCREAM FROSTING—

TIME: 5 MINUTES

A sweet and buttery crowd-pleaser that works with just about any cake!

1 STICK UNSALTED BUTTER, SOFTENED

4 CUPS CONFECTIONERS' SUGAR

3 TABLESPOONS MILK

1 TEASPOON PURE VANILLA EXTRACT

FOOD COLORING (OPTIONAL)

1) Place butter, sugar, milk, and vanilla in a large mixing bowl. Beat at low speed with an electric mixer to combine. Increase the speed to high, and beat for 2 minutes, or until light and fluffy. Add additional confectioners' sugar in 1-tablespoon increments if not stiff enough.

2) If tinting icing, transfer it to small cups and add food coloring, a few drops at a time, until desired color is reached. Stir well before adding additional coloring.

—CHOCOLATE BUTTERCREAM FROSTING—

TIME: 5 MINUTES

Our favorite frosting for birthday cakes and anything with chocolate, caramel, or coconut.

1 STICK UNSALTED BUTTER, SOFTENED

3 ½ CUPS CONFECTIONERS' SUGAR

½ CUPS UNSWEETENED COCOA POWDER

3 TABLESPOONS MILK

1 TEASPOON PURE VANILLA EXTRACT

1) Place butter, sugar, milk, cocoa and vanilla in a large mixing bowl. Beat at low speed with an electric mixer to combine.

2) Increase the speed to high, and beat for 2 minutes, or until light and fluffy. Add additional confectioners' sugar in 1-tablespoon increments if not stiff enough.

—CARAMEL SAUCE—

TIME: 5 MINUTES

This recipe isn't just limited to Bundt recipes. Caramel Sauce is also a great addition to ice cream sundaes, or just as a snack with apple slices!

1 CUP BROWN SUGAR

6 TABLESPOONS BUTTER

¼ CUP HALF AND HALF

1 TABLESPOON VANILLA

1) Mix the brown sugar, butter, and half and half together in a saucepan.

2) Cook over medium-low heat, whisking continuously, for about 5 minutes or until the sauce has thickened to desired consistency.

3) Remove from the heat, add the vanilla, and whisk until combined.

—STRAWBERRY SAUCE—

This sauce is an especially delicious accompaniment to Buttermilk Pound Cake.

2 CUPS STRAWBERRIES, SLICED

½ CUP SUGAR

1 TEASPOON VANILLA EXTRACT

1) Mix the strawberries, sugar, and vanilla together in a saucepan.

2) Cook over medium-low heat for about 10–15 minutes until the sauce thickens, stirring occasionally and mashing the strawberries lightly with a wooden spoon.

3) For a sauce with fewer strawberry chunks, puree in a blender to desired consistency.

–VANILLA PEACH COMPOTE–

TIME: 15 MINUTES

This compote's delicate, floral flavor adds a dash of elegance to any cake, but it's particularly delicious served over our Rosewater Pound Cake.

7 MEDIUM PEACHES, PEELED AND CHOPPED

1/4 CUP SUGAR

1/2 VANILLA BEAN, SCRAPED

2 TEASPOONS ROSEWATER (OPTIONAL)

1) Bring the peaches, sugar, vanilla bean and 1 teaspoon of rose water to a simmer for 10 minutes in a medium saucepan over medium heat.

2) Remove the saucepan from the heat and add the remaining teaspoon of rosewater. Transfer to a small bowl, set aside and allow to cool.

3) Serve over individual slices of cake.

–RASPBERRY LEMON SAUCE–

TIME: 5 MINUTES

This sauce is an especially delicious accompaniment to Buttermilk Pound Cake.

1 CUP RASPBERRY JAM

JUICE FROM 1/2 LEMON

PINCH OF SALT

FRESH RASPBERRIES, FOR GARNISH (OPTIONAL)

1) In a small saucepan, heat the raspberry jam for two minutes—just until the consistency loosens up.

2) Add lemon juice.

3) Pour over the whole cake or serve on individual slices. Add fresh raspberries for garnish.

Any soft fruits such
as berries or plums work
as a substitute for
the peaches.

Innovative Ideas:

FRUIT FILLING

Adding fruit to the center of a Bundt cake not only ensures that the fruit stays bright and fresh, but it also makes for a spectacular presentation. Including the decadence of fresh fruit makes any dessert feel like a special occasion.

BIRD FEEDER

Bundts actually make lovely bird feeders once you get them hanging. Naturally, they hold plenty of birdseed, so prepare to be very popular with your new winged friends. One method of doing this is to simply fill your Bundt pan with bird seed and suspend the pan from a tree branch with hooks and ropes.

The other version allows you to reuse your pan. Mix 1 package of unflavored gelatin with $\frac{1}{2}$ cup of warm water. Then whisk in $\frac{3}{4}$ cup all-purpose flour and 3 tbsp corn syrup. Next, mix the edible glue with 4 cups of bird food together. Spray your pan with nonstick cooking spray and press in the bird food mixture until firmly packed. Let it sit overnight and remove from the pan once set. Tie your bird seed wreath to a tree and enjoy!

S'MORES CONTAINER

Bring all the s'mores fixin's in one handy vessel. Fill the pan with graham crackers, chocolate, marshmallows, and long skewers for crisping the marshmallows just right.

Metric Conversions

US measurement	Approximate metric liquid measurement	Approximate metric dry measurement
1 teaspoon	5 mL	
1 tablespoon or ½ ounce	15 mL	14 g
1 ounce or ⅛ cup	30 mL	29 g
¼ cup or 2 ounces	60 mL	57 g
⅓ cup	80 mL	
½ cup or 4 ounces	120 mL	¼ pound/ 113 g
⅔ cup	160 mL	
¾ cup or 6 ounces	180 mL	
1 cup or 8 ounces or ½ pint	240 mL	½ pound/ 227 g
1 ½ cups or 12 ounces	350 mL	
2 cups or 1 pint or 16 ounces	475 mL	1 pound/ 454 g
3 cups or 1 ½ pints	700 mL	
4 cups or 2 pints or 1 quart	950 mL	

Pan Size Conversions

Standard Bundt Pans

Standard Bundt pans are around 10 inches in diameter and hold about 12 cups.

If you have a "small" Bundt pan that only holds 6-10 cups, start checking for doneness with a toothpick at least 10 minutes before the recommended bake time in the recipe.

If your Bundt pan holds more than 12 cups, you'll need to add about 5-10 minutes onto the recommended bake time. Check at the recommended time in the recipe, and continues to bake until a toothpick can be cleanly removed from the center.

Mini Bundts

Miniature Bundt pans typically have a 4-5 cup capacity. If you have a larger mini Bundt pan, you'll need to add 3-5 minutes onto your baking time. If you have a smaller mini Bundt pan, start checking for doneness at least 5 minutes before the recommended bake time in the recipe to prevent burning.

If you don't have a mini Bundt pan, you can substitute a doughnut pan or muffin tin and achieve similar results. Doughnut pans usually hold less batter than a mini Bundt does, so start checking 5-10 minutes before the recommended bake time. If you're using a muffin tin, be careful not to overfill. Fill each hole no more than three quarters of the way. Start checking about 5 minutes before the recommended time using a toothpick, but keep in mind that muffin versions can take less or more time depending on how filled they are.

No Bundt? No Problem!

If you don't have a Bundt pan handy, here are some alternatives that could be substituted for a standard Bundt pan.

9 x 13-inch baking pan

2 9-inch round cake pans

Because these pans will spread the batter out more, they will take less time to bake than a traditional Bundt would. Cut the recommended bake time in each recipe in half and start checking for doneness with a toothpick, continuing to bake as needed until the toothpick comes out clean.

Index

Acknowledgments

The Editors of Tide and Town would like to thank Sarah Guilbeaux, Evan Johnson, Jake Grogan, and Kelly Gauthier for their dedication and recipe contributions to this cookbook.

This book combines a variety of recipes and ideas that would not have been possible without the love and attention of publisher John Whalen, designers Jaime Christopher and Cindy Butler, editor Patrick Scafidi, and the Cider Mill Press team.

About Cider Mill Press
Book Publishers

Good ideas ripen with time. From seed to harvest, Cider Mill Press brings fine reading, information, and entertainment together between the covers of its creatively crafted books. Our Cider Mill bears fruit twice a year, publishing a new crop of titles each spring and fall.

"Where Good Books Are Ready for Press"

Visit us on the Web at
www.cidermillpress.com
or write to us at
PO Box 454
12 Spring St.
Kennebunkport, Maine 04046